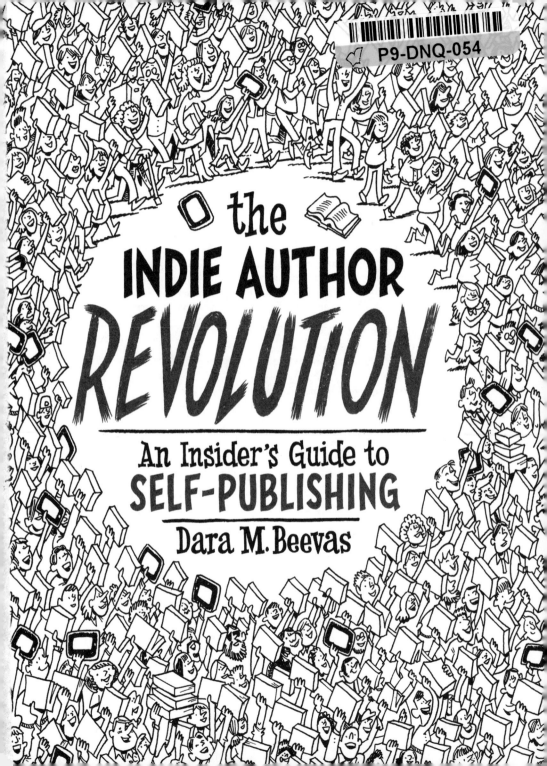

the INDIE AUTHOR REVOLUTION

An Insider's Guide to SELF-PUBLISHING

Dara M. Beevas

Paperback ISBN: 978-1-59298-504-3
E-book ISBN: 978-59298-505-0
Library of Congress Control Number: 2012916102

Cover illustration by Kevin Cannon
Page layout and design by Ryan Scheife, Mayfly Design
Typeset in Bembo

Printed in the United States of America
First Printing: 2013

17   16   15   14   13   5   4   3   2   1

Beaver's Pond Press, Inc.
7108 Ohms Lane, Edina, MN 55439-2129
(952) 829-8818 • www.BeaversPondPress.com

To order, visit www.BeaversPondBooks.com or call (800) 901-3480.
Reseller discounts available.

To all who fought to make self-publishing a respectable alternative. Thanks to you, good work is able to achieve its divine purpose.

To the inventor of the mentoring press, Milton "Beaver" Adams, who at age seventy decided to help authors reach beyond the "gatekeepers" to follow their passions and live their dreams.

To the authors who had the chutzpah to never give up!

Contents

Preface

In 1998, I dreamed (as many undergraduate English majors do) of a career in publishing: a lofty position working with a New York royalty publisher, relationships with awe-inspiring *New York Times*-bestselling authors, and a charming office where I would spend endless days and nights engrossed in good books. Almost fifteen years later, my dream is better than what I'd imagined. While the Minneapolis skyline is more subdued than that of New York City, I work with awe-inspiring authors who don't need the *New York Times* to be bestselling. And I do have that charming office lined with books. Not only are they award-winning, but they're also written by people who have become my friends. By taking the road less traveled, I was granted the opportunity to participate in the single-most remarkable phenomenon in publishing since the Internet.

When I get the occasional raised eyebrow from someone about my work, I don't take it personally. A distinguished professor I met a few years ago bit her upper lip and unabashedly frowned as I explained my job was mentoring indie authors and helping them self-publish. That same professor has since asked for my business card.

Times have changed, and what's even more incredible is that readers have changed with the times. We're in the age of the indie author. Books are no longer about the publisher—a good book is a good book no matter the method it came to print. I was once one of those harsh critics of self-publishing. Many authors I work with were once skeptics too. The thing about any phenomenon that shifts an industry and affects a cultural mainstay is that it catches everyone by surprise. In this business I've learned surprise is good, because once the surprise wears off, curiosity and innovation aren't far behind, and then comes the best part—the revolution.

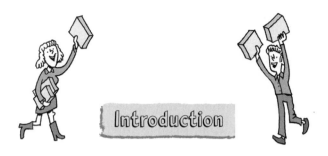

The Journey Begins...

I'm guessing that since you've picked up this book, you're interested in this thing called self-publishing. Maybe you talked to or heard about someone who self-published and wondered how the heck they figured it out. You may have thought: *What are the tricks? How do I self-publish a book that I will be proud of?* I've now worked with authors for more than a decade, and I've got answers to these questions. By the end of this book, you'll have the tips and tools needed to grow your publishing vision. You'll fully understand the steps and will be able to determine a strategy for how to create, market, and sell your book without going crazy. You'll become your own self-publishing guru, ready to make your dream of becoming an author a reality. Hopefully, you'll come to the conclusion I came to years ago: self-publishing is a powerful and innovative way for good content to break into the marketplace.

So what is self-publishing? Frankly, it has meant many things over the years—and the definition is still changing. Not too long ago, industry elites wrote off self-publishing as a quick and dirty solution for "rejects," manuscripts that for some reason didn't meet editorial expectations or market "needs." Thankfully, the publishing world is shifting, and so are perceptions about self-publishing and the benefits it brings to unknown authors. Many authors are even turning their backs on royalty publishing contracts. Barry Eisler, a best-selling author of thrillers, turned the publishing world upside down in March 2011 when he walked away from a two-book, half-million-dollar deal with St. Martin's Press. Instead, Eisler decided to self-publish his next book electronically.[1] Eisler's story is evident of an important time in publishing history—authors control their content and no longer depend upon publishers to determine their paths.

Today, the definition of self-publishing is putting your effort (including time, money, and skills) into producing a book. It is an author's personal investment of resources into his or her work from idea, to manuscript, to book. And as I see it, the best way to make such an investment worthwhile is to produce a high-quality, marketable book, one fit to rival any book produced by royalty-based publishers. To be successful at self-publishing, you must have high standards for every aspect of your book, from the editing, design, and printing to marketing and distribution. Books held to lower expectations are what gave self-publishing a negative reputation in the past. A book that looks or reads as if it has been "self-published" usually indicates shortcuts in editing, design, and printing, which traditional publishers are known for not taking. The

To be successful at self-publishing, you must have high standards for every aspect of your book, from the editing, design, and printing to marketing and distribution.

secret? You don't have to take shortcuts, either. Technologies for both desktop publishing software and online publishing tools have created an impression that writing and publishing are easy, which is not true. Beyond that, authors are not formally trained editors or designers and have no idea what they don't know. There are, however, tricks of the trade that will help indie authors make the right decisions without sacrificing quality or compromising their visions.

With self-publishing, you get what you put into it. Achieving quality demands attention and effort. Self-publishing requires hands-on collaboration between the author and those who have expertise in editing, proofreading, page layout, cover art, book production, printing, binding, distribution, and project management. The resources you choose should be reputable; your collaborators need to have working knowledge of publishing and the book world. Otherwise, you'll waste time, effort, and money on a book that won't make the cut. The "self" in "self-publishing" simply means that your book's success rests in your extremely capable hands.

How Self-Publishing Works

If you remember anything from this book, remember this: a first-time indie author is on a level playing field with a first-time traditionally published author. Traditional publishing houses' advances and debuts are down, and so are the marketing budgets for new authors.[2] When pairing this fact with the increasing power of the Internet and word of mouth, indie authors with valuable content have equal footing with unknown, traditionally published authors.

The Internet changed readers' relationships with authors, so that indie authors with a platform, a unique message, and timely content profit more from self-publishing. Further, technology has made self-publishing cheaper, faster, and easier. With the Information Age comes a new way of marketing and selling books. Get ready to shift your thinking from mounting a traditional publicity plan that makes your book a blockbuster, million-dollar seller complete with Oprah's recommendation to a strategy that requires grassroots marketing and reaching vast numbers of underserved audiences via the web. (I discuss PR and marketing at length in Chapter 10 and Chapter 11.)

Knowledge is power, and if you're making the decision to publish your book, be sure that readers will find value in it. Any book, self-published or not, is about giving the reader something to talk about, remember, learn from, and enjoy. An unforgettable book is not about the author at all—it's about satisfying the reader with valuable content. Today's consumers are drawn to information that enlightens, empowers, and engages. Authors must position their books by delivering useful experiences and information, and then market it strategically by targeting the right people at the right time. Understanding your audience and building an effective strategy to reach them is a must for success.

Learning What You Need to Know

I've written this book to help indie authors who wish to forge their own paths to success. Making the decision to self-publish feels overwhelming on one hand and irresistibly romantic on the other. Understandably, authors become nervous, anxious, and apprehensive about all that goes into publishing a book. It's also easy to fall into a dreamy-eyed reverie when you're thinking about TV appearances, interviews, book signings, social networking, book tours, and growing a readership. In the end, making thoughtful choices throughout the process saves time, money, and frustration and keeps you motivated to do the real work needed to produce a book.

My relationships with authors over the years have made me aware of the challenges they face. A writer interested in publishing a mystery romance or a self-help book will have focused, possibly for years, on crafting an engaging read. They have not invested the same time and interest on page layout, cover design, and printing costs. For this book, I have asked authors to describe their experiences for your benefit. I specifically requested them to share what they wished they'd known when they began their efforts, and these authors didn't hold back. You'll discover their advice is real, heartfelt, and without pretense. The ups and downs of self-publishing as experienced by authors, along with the perspective of someone who has managed the publishing process from start to finish (yours truly), will provide the information you need to go into self-publishing with your eyes wide open.

I've also incorporated feedback from professionals who help authors daily—editors, designers, book marketing experts, and bookstore managers. I've included their words of wisdom about building self-publishing as a successful venture given the challenges, changes, and opportunities in today's publishing climate. Use all of these true experiences to support your own publishing efforts.

If you're passionate and willing to embrace all that publishing has to offer, this book is for you. You'll meet interesting people, work with creative minds, inspire readers, and maybe even change lives.

PART I

LAUNCHING THE IDEA

Trust that little voice in your head that says "Wouldn't it be interesting if…" And then do it.

~Duane Michals, *More Joy of Photography*

To Publish or Not to Publish?

Over the years, more and more authors I've met have chosen to self-publish. Some knew from the beginning that the traditional publishing route wasn't for them. Others researched various options and decided that self-publishing was the right choice given their goals. Robin Dedeker, author of the memoir *Moments of Intuition*, explained, "I felt guided to look at all different kinds of publishing and spent a year researching. I really needed my book to speak my truth. I talked with other authors who published with royalty publishers, and their books were just shredded. I wanted my book to be my concept—my story—and so I knew it had to be self-published."

Robin felt strongly that her memoir about the power of using one's intuition was her story to tell, and she chose self-publishing in order to maintain her story's authenticity. Robin's sentiment is not uncommon. Establishing and maintaining control over content is a frequent reason authors explore self-publishing. As an indie author, you, too, will be hands-on in the creation and production of your book, and for many authors, this kind of control is not only important, but essential. Author Marilyn Jax, a mystery writer, put it this way: "As a newcomer to the fiction/mystery genre, I wanted to get my book out there and maintain control over my cover and interior design, and to retain all rights to my book."

The desire to sidestep the demoralizing limitations of traditional publishing is another huge reason authors choose to self-publish. Most first-time authors who reach out to agents and pursue royalty publishing wait months before receiving a response—good or bad. Frequently, the long, idle wait results in a rejection letter. In fact, countless authors share the experience of receiving not one, but several rejection letters. Author DeAnne Sherman, who coauthored three nonfiction books helping teens cope with difficult circumstances, said, "We were rejected by fifteen different publishers. We felt a strong calling to get these books in the market, knowing the need was there. We were certain that what we knew, no one else was writing." DeAnne and her daughter, Michelle Sherman, a clinical psychologist who works with children and families, have since gone on to

Most first-time authors who reach out to agents and pursue royalty publishing wait months before receiving a response—good or bad.

sell more than one hundred thousand copies of their books. The Shermans were confident that their books would meet a real need and that they had a ready market. The Shermans could see what the publishers could not, and by not giving up, they proved that they were right.

Like the Shermans, more and more authors have decided not to wait for agents and royalty publishers to validate their ideas, especially if they know that there is a call for their books to exist. Derek Wolden, who wrote *Basketcases: How Youth Basketball Parents Can Lower Their Blood Pressure and Keep Their Sanity*, is one such author. "I thought self-publishing would be the best route because I was writing to such a niche audience. I was rejected by several agents and encountered lots of roadblocks." Like the Shermans, he was proven right.

Whatever your reasons for self-publishing, be true to the confidence you have in your book's potential. Empower yourself with as much information about self-publishing as possible. In the words of author Robin Dedeker,

> *Your book should be so important to you that you couldn't live without publishing it. It has to be as important to your life as breathing, because it requires a great deal of work and dedication. Be willing to make sacrifices. There has to be such ownership when you self-publish. You have to believe in your work. If you only sell a few hundred books, you have to believe that going through the publishing process was valuable in its own right.*

These words are honest and true, and they hint at more: deciding to self-publish requires thinking, writing, publishing, and marketing outside the box. Remember, rejection happens for a reason. When editors and agents don't believe in a book, they won't take it on. When you're self-publishing, you must believe in your book. If you don't believe in it, your book has no chance.

How to Know if You're On to Something

Let me guess: A fully-formed idea keeps you up at night, or a vague feeling comes and goes, nagging you to pursue it and explore how far you could take it. For some reason, you can't shake the sense that you've got a book in you. I know the feeling. And if you're like me, at any given moment you feel a combination of excitement, fear, and self-doubt. You've probably asked yourself, *Can I really do this? Should I really do this?* You've wondered—or even obsessed about—whether your idea could make the cut. For the record, you're not alone. Lots of folks, including myself, have been there.

The truth is that not every idea makes a terrific book. Even the good ideas might not be unique enough to penetrate today's competitive market. Sadly, many authors have had to learn painful lessons after they've made the decision (and investment) to publish. Having a great idea doesn't mean that you should necessarily write and publish a manuscript. However, there's good news: a plethora of great ideas have produced brilliant books. Your book idea could (and hopefully will) fall into that category. But how do you know if your idea would make a good book?

Before you decide to publish your book, ask yourself, *Why does it need to be published?* One author (let's call her Carol) wrote a memoir. Carol experienced a troubled childhood, and following a tumultuous divorce, found herself in a second abusive relationship. She used writing as a way to get through these painful experiences. The resulting manuscript shared her life's twists and turns in grim detail. Carol's book from start to finish was every awful thing that had happened to her in a twenty-year span. While writing helped Carol cope and recover from her difficult life circumstances, the manuscript itself suffered several challenges. For one, Carol's storytelling skills weren't the best—and for a memoir, storytelling is critical. Her story was also not unique or engrossing, which meant she couldn't make a strong case to readers about why they should care about her life or what they would get from reading about it. Every book has to answer the universal reader's question, *What's in it for me?*

> **Every book has to answer the universal reader's question, *What's in it for me?***

Without a laudable voice and a rich story, there's nothing for the reader to grab a hold of. Readers crave value from any book—including yours—and they want to experience an "ah ha" moment. Think about *why* you want to publish your book, *who* you think will read your book, and *why* that particular audience *needs* you to publish your book. Even further, what would a reader *not* find interesting about your book? Authors who take these questions to heart frequently find success. Time and again, I've encountered authors who have self-published to fulfill a specific need or speak to an equally specific audience and found the success they were hoping for. This is common with authors who looked for books on particular subjects and couldn't find them. Their solution: writing and publishing the books they couldn't find.

Such was the case for Amy Recob, who searched for a children's picture book about food allergies. She simply couldn't find one that talked about all the main food allergies children often suffer. So, she created *The Bugabees: Friends with Food Allergies* series, working with a top-shelf graphic design firm to create wonderful illustrations. She has since sold several thousand copies. Doctors, nurses, parents, and educators are thankful for her books—and so are kids. The books have helped countless children feel better about being deprived of everyday foods that other kids enjoy.

In the publishing world, I've come across thousands of people (probably more) who, like Amy, know they have valid ideas. Some have vast potential, while others require more careful thought. Even after determining that you 1) have the means and resources to skillfully write your book and 2) have a book that is in fact marketable, you'll then have to 3) figure out whether you have the time, commitment, and chutzpah to reach your audience. If all these factors come together, go for it!

Here's a checklist to determine whether you're on to an idea that's suitable for developing into a self-published book:

- ☐ You have observed and heard others say that your idea targets an untapped audience in need of your book.
- ☐ You have a business or are launching one, and your book would educate or inspire your clients.
- ☐ Your business clients frequently request additional or supplemental materials to support the presentations, training, or seminars you offer.
- ☐ You've worked hard to hone your writing skills and have received positive feedback on your work from writing professionals.
- ☐ You're closely connected to a topic or cause and have an existing relationship with others who are also connected.

☐ You're a known and respected resource or expert on a specific topic to appreciative audiences.

☐ Your writing has been featured or showcased for its skillfulness and creativity.

☐ Your idea provides a fresh take on a familiar topic.

If you checked two or more of the above, then your idea is probably a good candidate for a book. If you don't know where to begin, join a writing workshop where you can share your ideas (and possibly your manuscript) with other writers. Writing workshops and classes are smart ways to receive unbiased, valuable feedback and insight about your book idea's originality. Note: Friends and family members are rarely good resources for honest, unbiased feedback! Count on them for encouragement, not for constructive criticism.

It's no secret that writing is probably the most important part of your journey as an author. But the writing process is simply that: a process. Don't be intimidated. At times the words will flow out of you, and at other times they won't. Most authors find that writing requires tremendous discipline, which means writing even when they don't feel like it. In my experience, the biggest enemy for determined writers is self-doubt. Don't talk yourself out of writing your book. It will certainly be a roller-coaster ride of emotions throughout—I promise you that—but with dedication, the rewards will outweigh the difficulties.

Enlighten, Empower, and Engage:
The Formula for a Successful Book

When meeting new authors, I often hear stories about how they came to write and pursue the self-publication of their books. I've heard it all, from how a book idea appeared to an author in the middle of the night to how inspiration stemmed from a unique life experience. As a result, it's my belief that every successful idea has what I call the power of the "Three Es": it enlightens, empowers, and engages. Good books provide insight about a subject, topic, or experience; that is, they *enlighten*. A great book *empowers* readers with information they didn't know or a perspective they didn't have. Finally, a truly strong book draws readers in; it *engages* them so they become invested in the story or the book's message. The Three Es play a critical part in the marketing of books, too. As we'll see later, they help get a book into the hands of the right audience. Paying attention to the Three Es will help you transform an initial idea into a powerful force. It will guide you toward doing what's most important, beginning with writing the best book possible. It all goes back to and begins with a remarkable story. In the words of marketing expert Sara Lien, owner of Lien Public Relations:

> *The public is looking for an intriguing, well-written story. So are journalists! When writing your book, think about your audience first. The media will organically find your book if your audience is intrigued.*

Sara is right—it's all about the intrigue, and if your book incorporates the Three Es, you'll be on the right path.

If You Could Wave a Magic Wand...

The first question I pose to new indie authors is, "If you could wave a magic wand, what would your book be and what would it do for readers?" I ask this because the successful indie author is goal-oriented, sets realistic objectives, and commits to reaching them. For instance, your goal may be to raise awareness about a specific topic or to promote a new approach to business leadership. Keeping that goal in front of you will increase your success. Tim Munkeby, author of *If I Had a Million Dollars,* shared, "My objective was to educate young adults on fiscal responsibility so they wouldn't make the same financial mistakes as the generations before them." But not all goals lead authors where they want to go. If, for example, your motivation for self-publishing is financial or you're looking to become instantly famous, you'll probably be disappointed. The authors who genuinely care about their content and decide that getting rich isn't the goal are the ones who surpass their financial expectations in the end.

If you look at the nonfiction books that consistently sell the most copies, you'll notice that many are categorized as self-help, business, personal finance, relationship, and diet/fitness. Think about the common thread that attracted these books to buyers. They likely offered "the promise" of solving a problem. I've discovered that in today's book

> **Authors who provide genuine value in their books surpass those who don't.**

market, buyers seek solutions more than ever before. Authors who provide genuine value in their books surpass those who don't. Of course, in order to address the problems that need to be solved, you'll need to become familiar with your audience, think like them, and understand what they would consider a solution, improvement, or, as in fiction, an entertaining read. What enlightens, empowers, and engages your audience? To succeed, you need to know.

In essence, today's authors have to be ambitious and innovative, and they constantly need to be thinking outside the box—and outside the bookstore. You have to grab and keep the attention of a public whose attention span is shrinking. And let's face it—today's books have to compete with television, computers, MP3 players, smartphones, and tablets. With technology and information at everyone's fingertips, it's critical that, as you work through the content of your book, you continue to honestly assess if your book accomplishes those Three Es.

Authors have adapted to today's environment by accepting the fact that, in addition to being authors, they also have to be publicists, speakers, event planners, bloggers, promoters, columnists, and entertainers. In fact, this is true for every author across every avenue of publishing. I don't say this to intimidate you; in my experience, it's not as scary as it sounds. The wonderful thing about marketing a book is that you've already done the research, compiled the content, and written the masterpiece. Stepping into your new roles simply requires drawing on all of that creativity to attract your audience. In the words of Marilyn Jax,

Be prepared and motivated to work hard to get out there and sell your book on a rather constant basis. If you're passionate about writing and marketing, then go for it! Like anything else in life that is worthwhile, it is a lot of work. Successful authors are not made overnight. An author must put in his or her time. It is a process. Self-publishing has its challenges, but for me, it has been an enriching experience.

You, along with the people who will help publish your book, should think about your short- and long-term self-publishing goals from the beginning. When it comes to jumpstarting your plan and defining your goals, you'll need to decide the following:

- **What is your vision?** What do you specifically want to achieve with your book? An example would be, "I want to provide real estate agents with alternative methods to market and sell houses in a seller's market."

- **Who will work with you?** Who will be responsible for the editing, design, and production of the book? The following professionals typically get involved: editors, illustrators, book designers, proofreaders, printers, project managers, accountants, distributors, online publishing help, website designers, and publicists.

- **How will you market your book and reach your goals?** How do you plan to get your name out there? How will you raise awareness? What will you do to get your book in the hands of those who need to read it? An example of a strategy would be to focus on direct sales through events targeted to your audience (For example, craft shows, music festivals, or flea markets) and to target retailers that attract your audience.

- **When is the right time to launch your book to best accomplish your goals?** When should your book hit the market to have the most impact? For example, you might want to have your book coincide with a holiday, special event, an annual fundraiser, season, sales opportunity (for example, Great Outdoors Month), or an anniversary related to your book topic. Tip: For a complete list of "special months" go to the Wikipedia website (www.wikipedia.org) and search for "list of observances in the United States by presidential proclamation."

- **Will your book enlighten, empower, and engage your audience?** How will you accomplish and leverage the Three Es to build relationships with your audience and develop your national profile? As a suggestion, visit a local networking group and give a presentation on your book's subject. If your audience is engaged throughout the presentation, asks lots of questions, requests supporting or accompanying materials, and would have bought a book had it been available, chances are your book has relationship-building potential.

THE LAST WORD

- Investigate your book idea's potential. Will it deliver the "ah ha" factor? Be realistic when you contemplate why you think it should be published.
- Books that enlighten, empower, and engage readers are better positioned to attract a following and sustain momentum once published. Will your book do that?
- Become an expert on your book's topic and its audience. Understand your book's value and how you'll deliver it to readers before you begin the self-publishing process.

💡 Indie Author Wisdom

"I didn't write the book so it would become a best-seller. I wanted it to help me gain credibility, be a resource for my clients, and be something I could offer at events. The traditional publishing route didn't hold much value for me for those reasons."

~Deirdre Van Nest, speaker and performance coach for professional service providers, author of *Fire Your Fear: How to Grow Your Business by Changing the Way You Think*

Chapter 2

Self-Publishing 101

So you've decided your book idea should come to life, and self-publishing may be for you. If you've researched self-publishing, you've likely come across phrases like *subsidy publishing, print-on-demand,* and *vanity publishing.* Self-publishing is a road traveled by scores of people, and the Internet is replete with a monumental number of companies looking to help people like you. All this information can be confusing. You might ask yourself, for example, what a vanity publisher is or how a vanity press differs from a print-on-demand company. And even further, you may not know if either is right for you.

Historically speaking, publishing a book through a vanity press has the most negative connotation in the publishing industry. The term "vanity" stems from the notion that an author who works with such a press does so for narcissistic reasons. I discourage working with vanity presses because they are known for providing little to no quality control and will likely not provide strategic direction for your book beyond helping you print it. In fact, by definition, a vanity press prints exactly what you give them. As a result, books produced by vanity presses usually don't receive important professional editing. Because of this, as well as other factors, these books carry the stigma of being amateur.

Many authors we respect today chose to publish their own books by means that closely resemble the vanity presses of today. Mark Twain, Upton Sinclair, Virginia Woolf, and Carol Lewis are just a few examples. Today, however, many vanity presses are known in the literary world for not being selective and for printing anything, regardless of

POD (Print-On-Demand): A digital printing technology suitable for small runs (twenty to five hundred book copies) printed and bound in much less time than traditional printing and binding methods.

Vanity Press: A company that helps authors self-publish, offering book design and printing services for a fee regardless of quality and marketability.

Mentoring Press: A hybrid publisher that guides authors with marketable manuscripts through the self-publishing process. Mentoring presses offer services for a fee that includes coaching, editing, book design, printing, publicity, and distribution. Mentoring presses are often selective and emphasize the importance of editing and good design to create successful books.

quality. This fact is why self-published authors with books from vanity presses typically have a hard time getting their work into stores and libraries. Even if a particular author's work is strong, it's tarnished by the poor reputations that vanity presses have in the industry.

Working with vanity presses yields other problems, such as having restrictive contracts that limit an author's ability to print their books elsewhere. Some vanity presses own the copyright of an author's book. Self-publishing should mean that you, the author, hold 100 percent of the rights to your book. If you do consider working with a vanity press, do a Google search to discover customers' experiences.

> **Self-publishing should mean that you, the author, hold 100 percent of the rights to your book.**

Working with a self-publishing company or mentoring press is not the same as working with a vanity press. Such companies will assist you with quality editing, book design, illustration, proofreading, and printing. In fact, self-publishing companies, often referred to as "mentoring presses" and "contract publishers," are in the business to help you produce a quality book—that is, if they are good at what they do. Traditionally, they don't take royalties on your book sales but do join forces with you to help you market your books.

To help with the decision of working with a self-publishing company or working with a vanity press, I suggest that you create a plan that incorporates quality as the driving factor for every publishing decision (see Publishing Plan in Appendix C). Bookstores, readers, and distributors will only pay attention to books that provide value, and this includes the look and feel of your book. It pays to do the work, do your research, and make decisions that result in a quality book, regardless of the direction you ultimately take.

- Advantages of a self-publishing company or mentoring press:
  1. **Control**: Authors usually direct content, editing, cover design, and timing.
  2. **Speed**: Self-publishing reduces time-to-market by months or even years.
  3. **Flexibility**: You can choose what works best for your budget, timeline, and creative vision throughout the publishing process.
  4. **Creative marketing opportunities**: You're only limited by your imagination—with you in the driver's seat, you'll discover limitless ways to reach your audience.
  5. **Larger profit potential**: You won't share royalties with a publisher, so you'll collect a greater profit per sale.
- Disadvantages of a self-publishing company or mentoring press:
  1. **Overwhelming**: You make all decisions and are responsible for executing each detail, including who you hire to help.
  2. **Steep learning curve**: You don't know what you don't know, and the publishing process includes several steps that might feel foreign.

3. **Distribution challenges**: Bookstores, whole-salers, and online book retailers have different requirements and often refuse to work with authors who don't have an established company that quickly processes orders.

4. **Red tape and administrative details**: The steps it takes to jumpstart book publishing, such as acquiring an ISBN and Library of Congress Control Number, feel tedious and time consuming.

5. **Unknowns hurt you economically**: Making a misstep anywhere in the process increases costs, which cuts into profit.

Publishing Solo versus Hiring a Self-Publishing Company

Could you self-publish completely on your own, without help from either a company or vanity press? Absolutely. Research the various resources, such as printing companies (not to be confused with book publishers) and online, on-demand book production companies like Amazon's CreateSpace. Books about self-publishing (like this one) will also help produce a quality book. It's definitely worth your time to find out what's out there.

You also have the option of working with a mentoring press, a company of book publishing professionals ready to work with you to meet your publishing goals. Both ways work. Think of either approach as renovating a house: You could shoulder the task of hiring and managing all the workers you need, or you could hire a contractor to do it for you. It depends on how involved you want to be in the process and whether you have the time, energy, and patience to go at it alone, without assistance and insider knowledge. Like anyone facing a complicated project, you'll want to talk with people who've tackled both options so you'll know what questions to ask throughout the publishing process.

Going solo means spending more time completing administrative tasks, searching for the right resources, and learning the process as you go. For the rare breed of author, this is a satisfying experience; truly "self-publishing." But not everyone has the time that it takes to go full indie. Most indie authors need and prefer the assistance and expertise of book publishing companies with skilled project managers, editors, designers, illustrators, ghostwriters, proofreaders, printers, and publicists at the ready.

> **Most indie authors need and prefer the assistance and expertise of book publishing companies, with skilled project managers, editors, designers, illustrators, ghostwriters, proofreaders, printers, and publicists at the ready.**

Author Tim Munkeby puts it this way: "If you can afford it, hiring a self-publishing company will most likely get your book produced quicker and with a lot less angst and frustration." Whether you go solo or hire a company, remember that quality is important. Do your research beforehand. Don't fall into the trap of becoming so excited about your book that you don't ask around for the best resources available.

If you decide to work with a mentoring publisher, you can choose to work with an online company, or one at a physical location that you can visit. Companies offer different services and charge differently for the services they offer. Some companies, for instance, charge by the hour for editing services, while others might charge by the word. In my experience, it's smarter to choose editors on the basis of experience and personality than on how they charge. Also, if you're looking to have your book available to book retailers such as Barnes & Noble, you need a company that assists with distribution, warehousing, and fulfillment services. Many companies charge extra for the added work to list a book with wholesalers like Ingram and Baker & Taylor.

The best advice for selecting the right self-publishing company is to get your hands on examples of books published through these companies. Do they look professionally produced? Can you tell that the books have been professionally edited? Are people at the company willing to share names and contact information for authors with whom they've worked? Can you find their books in bookstores? If they're not on the shelves, can you order them? Can you find the books listed with online retailers? Can you find media coverage about their books?

If there's a reputable bricks and mortar publishing company in your area, meet with them. You'll learn a lot by making face-to-face contact. If they pass muster, hire them! There's no substitute for the personal attention you get when you walk into your project manager's office and ask for a progress update. When you make a connection with your publisher, they're naturally more interested in you and more invested in your book.

Ultimately, you need to know what you want from a self-publishing company. Think about what matters most to you and ask yourself these questions to help narrow down your options:

1. Am I more comfortable working with a local company, or working online with a company located in another city, or in cyberspace? (And, based on my location, and my schedule, do I have a choice?)
2. Do I want to be involved in every step, or just the major decisions, or do I want someone to simply "handle it" for me?
3. Do I want my book offered nationwide, or am I realistically publishing for a smaller local audience?
4. What are my feelings about e-books and print books? Is my book more suited to be one or the other?
5. How am I funding this? What is my budget?
6. Is this book time-sensitive? What is my deadline?

Here are questions to ask any prospective publisher *before* making a decision:

1. How much involvement am I expected and allowed to have in the publishing process?
2. Will I be collaborating directly with editors, illustrators, and designers? How much is done in person, and how much via phone and e-mail? How accessible is my team?
3. What's the main strength of this company: price, speed, quality, simplicity, or a collaborative process?
4. What are my options for print and for e-books?
5. How long will it take?

6. What can I expect to pay, and when? (Get clear estimates and timelines.)

7. Tell me about your marketing, distribution, and warehousing procedures.

8. Are there authors who've done projects similar to mine who'd be willing to talk to me about their experience working with your company?

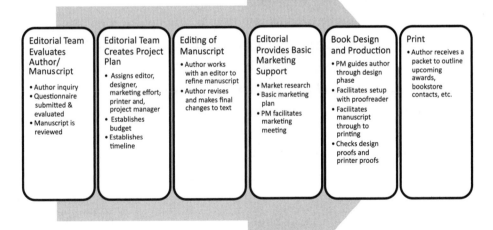

The Publishing Process for Indie Authors Working With a Hired Company

As you ask these questions, you'll get a good sense of which company's priorities are most aligned with your own. You'll come across many helpful resources when you begin your research in earnest. If you decide to go with a company, choose the company that will carry your book from idea to final product with your vision constantly in mind.

How to Know if a Publishing Expert Is a True Expert

I often meet authors who have spent pretty pennies getting their books published only to be disappointed by the end results. It's usually the case that the author trusts a person or service to deliver on the promise of publishing a book and bringing it to market. In the end, the company doesn't deliver—in one way or another. Sometimes the book is put together haphazardly and doesn't look professional. In other cases, companies don't follow through on promised services such as customized printing or adequate distribution, leaving the author with a product that's nearly impossible to sell.

Sometimes, sadly, companies inadequately advise an author about the quality of his or her manuscript and bring a poorly written and unedited (or poorly edited) book to print. Publishing professionals often won't honestly discuss the quality of a manuscript's writing with an author who needs to hear it. They're happy to take the author's money, print an unfinished book, and let the author worry about quality when it's too late. Avoid this pitfall by working on the writing extensively with a professional editor, or even multiple editors, before taking your manuscript to a publishing expert. There's not a professional writer anywhere who doesn't go through the invaluable process of editing to ensure clarity, accuracy, and focus in their manuscript. If you take a look at the Acknowledgments section of this book, you'll see that several professional editors had a hand in refining this book. I produced the content, and editors provided feedback, without altering my original voice. The result is a better book—more detailed, thorough, and prepared for publication with professional attention to matters of style. If you rush your incomplete or unedited work into the publishing process, you could find yourself wishing later that you had spent the extra time to hone your writing first.

On the plus side, many companies now work with indie authors. There's something out there for everybody, and options abound. Do your research and make an informed decision that aligns with your goals. As I recommended earlier, figure out what's important to you and establish what you're truly looking for. Then determine if the person or company you're interested in is truly a publishing expert. **Here are some signs that may indicate they're not:**

1. They've only been in the publishing industry six months to a year.
2. They can't show you samples of books they've published or helped publish.
3. They call themselves an expert, but there's no evidence that anyone else does.
4. When they're discussing strategy with you, they fail to mention either editing, distribution, or marketing.
5. Their background is in one area, such as website design, marketing, editing, or printing.
6. They ask for money without explaining in detail what it pays for.

7. They spend most of the time talking (or selling) and little time getting to know you or what your book is about.

8. They make grandiose promises of being able to help you sell millions of copies or make your book a best seller.

9. Books they've published aren't books that you would buy due to poor editing, print quality, or lack of accessibility.

10. Books they've worked on haven't been successful in the market.

Ask for referrals, and talk to multiple experts. Be aware of what you sincerely want and need—be honest about this from the beginning. If you are, you'll determine who's the right fit for your book, making it much harder for someone to take advantage of you. Think of it this way: Isn't it an affirming joy when you go to the grocery store with a shopping list? You know what you need and you're less likely to pick up things that you don't. Even better, you're likely to go to the right store that has all the things on your list. So make your list, and go shopping.

The Book Publishing Process in a Nutshell

Every book's publishing process is a little different, depending on how well-developed the manuscript is, whether it's fiction or nonfiction, if it includes photos, if it is intended for mass-market or specialty sales, and many other factors. The process will be different depending on whether you hire help or publish completely on your own. Either way, it's important to be aware of the steps in publishing so that you maintain control over the way your book develops and have confidence that it's being handled with care. As you approach publishing, create a schedule or timeline to track progress. If you're working with a mentoring publisher, they will help you with this.

In my experience, if an author isn't on a timeline or connected to the important dates throughout the process, the project takes a back seat to more immediate things in the author's life and loses priority. If you know where your book is in the publishing process and what the next steps are, you keep not only yourself accountable, but the people you've selected to help you. Here's my breakdown of a general publishing process, along with a timeline, that works well for indie authors. This particular process assumes that your manuscript is in final draft form and ready for the publishing process:

The Publishing Process for Indie Authors Working Without a Hired Company

1. **Prepublication Review (two to four weeks):** Before you ever enter the publishing process, have a professional editor review your manuscript. A review will help you evaluate the manuscript's focus, clarity, marketability, and editorial needs. The review will also assist you in making final changes before formally beginning.

2. **Project Management (ongoing):** This part of the process includes preliminary brainstorming on how to develop your business and marketing plan, the hiring of your publishing team, preparation for the book launch, finalizing back-cover copy, creating the biography, website development, and other processes.

3. **Editing (typically fifteen to thirty-five hours spread over two to six weeks):** This is the official first step in publishing. Editing is a process in which a professional editor reads a manuscript and evaluates it for grammar, syntax, voice, clarity, focus, organization, style, and other factors, and then recommends changes, additions, and deletions. Children's books typically take fewer hours of editing (usually three to six hours) than standard adult trade (or mass-market) books. An editor provides a cost estimate for your approval before he or she begins working. Editing is a collaborative process in which the editor places foremost priority on maintaining the author's vision and voice. Be prepared: A good editor will shed light on any problems in your manuscript. You may need (or want) to make substantive changes to your text, or to hunt down bet-

ter sources and citations. Build in time for yourself to do some re-writing after the editor hands back the document.

4. **Design (typically six to eight weeks):** Once the editing stage is complete, the design process follows. Ideally, the author and designer work together on the cover design and layout of the interior pages. It usually takes six to eight weeks for a designer to provide an estimate, create design proposals and mock-ups, typeset the manuscript, and create charts or other graphic elements.

5. **Proofreading (two to three weeks from final typeset pages):** Proofreading occurs during the design process and involves a professional proofreader reviewing a finished manuscript for errors in punctuation, spelling, and consistency. Professional proofreading ensures that your book meets the standards of the trade (mass market).

6. **Printing (softcover books typically require four to six weeks; hardcover books typically require six to eight weeks):** Following design, choose a high-quality book printer who will provide the best printing and binding services. Get quotes from at least three printers. Don't limit yourself to your own state; costs vary and it's worth shopping around.

7. **Distribution/Warehousing/Fulfillment (four weeks before the books are delivered to the printer):** This stage involves contacting bookstores and wholesalers about distribution, and establishing an order fulfillment plan. At this stage, you'll also list your book on Amazon

.com and take steps to register your book with Ingram and/or Baker & Taylor, two national wholesalers, to make your book available to bookstores. These companies are international registries that bookstores contact to order books. They are the umbrella over the entire commercial book business. If you decide to coordinate working with Baker & Taylor and Ingram without help from a self-publishing company, you will still need to partner with a company like Lightning Source (www.lightningsource .com) or Greenleaf Book Group (www.greenleafbook group.com), as both Baker & Taylor and Ingram primarily work with publishers of ten or more titles.

8. **Promotion (ongoing):** To make your book accessible to the public, you'll need to consider your promotional efforts as soon as possible. Consider your release date early on because newly released books often have to change hands a few times before reaching readers. The average book takes anywhere from six months to two years to produce. If you're looking to reach vast audiences, ensure the distribution is worked out in advance. If you know your book will be back from the printer on a certain date, make sure that your official "release" is at least a month later.

Key Publishing Terms to Remember

It's good to know the basics before getting too far into the process, so here are some general functions, terms, and keywords defined:

Author: The person who creates the original content and concept of the book. Even if a work is ghostwritten, the author is the person whose idea shapes and forms the book.

Publisher: The party who produces the book and makes it available for purchase through distributors, wholesalers, direct buyers, or other means. The publisher and author may be one and the same.

Distributor: Most easily described as the "middle men." Without a distributor, you'll be responsible for storing, shipping, and making your book available to wholesalers, retailers, and libraries. Another important value of distributors is that they make it possible for retail-

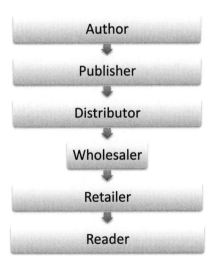

How a Book Typically Travels from Author to Reader

ers and wholesalers to return unsold books. If your book is not returnable, bookstores won't carry your book. Distributors don't purchase books; they distribute them to the channels that do. In essence, distributors hold books on consignment. Distribution is a service that many self-publishing companies offer.

Wholesaler: This is a company that acts as the repository for retailers, businesses, online bookstores, and libraries. A wholesaler buys books at a discount, usually from a publisher's distributor, and then makes them available to the market. Wholesalers are viewed in the industry as "one-stop shops" for book retailers. They make it convenient for retailers to buy inventory from a central place rather than buying books from thousands of book distributors. They also make returns possible, which is a requirement for book retailers. The two largest book wholesalers in the country are Ingram and Baker & Taylor.

Book Retailers: These are stores that stock their shelves with books purchased from authors, publishers, distributors, and wholesalers. However, bigger retail chains (like Barnes & Noble) almost exclusively purchase through wholesalers like Ingram or Baker & Taylor. Book retailers range from huge to small, from chain to independent, and include gift shops, grocery stores, and emporiums of every variety.

- If you're hoping to take your book national or even international, avoid vanity presses that print exactly what you give them without enforcing quality checks. Also partner with a publisher or distributor who works with Ingram and Baker & Taylor.
- Know what you want before publishing. This will help you decide what publishing route is best for you, regardless of sales pitches designed to get your business.
- When you finish your manuscript, entrust it to a professional editor to ensure its readiness for publication. Then make all major tweaks before it enters the publishing process.
- Do your research. Don't work with the first publisher you encounter until you've checked out other options. Ask questions. Request examples for references and evidence of proven success.

Indie Author Wisdom

"My advice to authors is to know your audience as precisely as you can before you start writing."

~Gordon Fredrickson, award-winning children's book author of the Farm Country and If I Were a Farmer series

Chapter 3

Starting with the Plan

A smart approach to publishing your book is to position it from the beginning as a business, regardless of your genre. The goal of most authors is to have copies of their books in the hands of interested readers. Viewing your book as the cornerstone of a business with a thoughtful strategy to reach your goals is a crucial first step on the road to success. It's the publisher who leads the business, so as an indie author, you're in charge. Your book's success rests in your own hands, and positioning your book as the foundation of a business means that you commit to the following:

- Plan for your book's long-term growth with a written publishing plan.
- Decide how to best fulfill the plan.
- Establish your book's purpose and niche.
- Identify a platform on which to launch and market your book.
- Find the right partners to help you fulfill the plan.

Every successful self-published author will tell you that publishing means planning. You wouldn't open a restaurant without a plan, would you? You shouldn't publish your book without one, either. It doesn't have to be an extensive hundred-page document. Start small, asking the simple question: *Why am I creating my book?* Your plan is the foundation as you navigate through the publishing process. Creating a blueprint for how you want to pursue your book's development will keep you grounded and tied to objectives rather than acting on mere emotional impulses.

When you think about what makes a business successful, consider what convinced the marketplace that it was indispensable and unique. This applies to books, too. Books that solve problems experienced by many will do better than books written for self-serving reasons.

> **Books that solve problems experienced by many will do better than books that were written for self-serving reasons.**

Remember our earlier example of Carol's blundering memoir? From the moment you've made the decision to publish your book, ask yourself why a reader would want to buy it. What's your case for why your book should be published? Remember, the reason self-publishing has had a bad rap is because of the misconception that everyone who self-publishes is a reject. This is not true. A major reason self-published authors do well is that they reach audiences that the major publishing houses have passed over. Your book should answer a question, fill a void in the marketplace, or present a fresh story with a fresh voice. Have a book that your readers will feel grateful for having found and read. Then make all this clear in a publishing plan.

Consider this: To publish a book traditionally, the first thing you do after completing the manuscript is write a book proposal that makes a case to agents and publishers for why it should be in print. As a self-publisher, make the case to yourself! You're the publisher, you're the investor, and you need a plan to successfully market your own book. Just like McGraw-Hill, Penguin, or any of the other major publishers, you must know why your book should be in print and what makes it worthy of the investment required for its success.

Your publishing plan should identify your mission statement, sales objectives, market, and competing titles. It should include a book summary, marketing strategies, your biography, and your audience profiles. Later, when you put together your marketing plan, much of this information will be valuable. A plan is also necessary to acquire financial help, either from investors or a financial institution. No matter what, by creating your publishing plan, you'll be empowered and jazzed about the future of your book. You'll find a sample publishing plan in the appendix section of this book for your reference.

It's All About the Niche: Developing Your Publishing Purpose Statement

Successful authors, especially self-publishing ones, should have a purpose; your next step is informing readers of that purpose. The place to start is with a mission statement, or as I like to call it, a "publishing purpose statement." Don't worry about it changing in the future. It probably will. Start with something as basic as "Educating readers about (fill in the blank)," or "Entertaining readers with a ripping good mystery," or, in one author's case, "Using earth-conscious images to teach ABCs to preschoolers." That last purpose statement does three things well. It identifies a unique approach (earth-conscious images), includes its educational value (teaching the alphabet), and targets a niche market (preschoolers). Colleen Baldrica, award-winning author of *Tree Spirited Woman,* said the following about her publishing purpose: "I want my book to prompt people to reflect on their lives. I want my readers to be able to read it anytime and receive exactly what they need at that very moment."

Ask yourself: What is my calling, and how does my book serve to meet my calling? Constructing a purpose statement around your answer will give your book the foundation it needs to stay afloat in today's marketplace. Author Derek Wolden knew he was filling a need from the outset: "I wrote *Basketcases* for the right reasons. It was written purely for a niche audience. There was nothing like it in the country, and I'm an expert on the topic." As an experienced basketball official who had suffered at the hands of irate and misinformed parents, he knew there was a market for his book on proper spectator behavior in youth basketball. So far, he's met market demand with several thousand copies of his book.

Your purpose statement should be the exciting reason why your book is important to publish. Suzanne Ruff's book *The Reluctant Donor* is a memoir about donating a kidney to save her sister from polycystic kidney disease (PKD). Suzanne shared that her book's mission was "to prompt awareness about PKD and ignite a passion to seek a cure." That is to say, she saw her book's mission as spreading the word about her family's experience, building awareness and educating people about PKD, and influencing people to support and find a cure.

Your purpose statement doesn't have to go on and on. And it certainly doesn't need to be—and shouldn't be—in "corporate language" that gives your project a false air of self-importance. As in most areas related to creating a book, with purpose statements, less is definitely more. Begin with the effect you want your book to have on its reader, and I guarantee you'll come up with ideas from there. If your book is designed to inspire, help, or educate, your purpose statement should say so. Mystery novelist Marilyn Jax says her mission is "to write quality, page-turner mysteries without graphic gore and gratuitous sex—compelling stories that leave the reader awed by the experience of the read, and begging for the next one."

Also remember that purpose drives content. Let's say you're writing about starting a small business. If you're writing to entertain, you might include stories about hilarious mistakes new entrepreneurs make. If you're writing to motivate, you'd include information about what makes starting a small business worthwhile. If you're writing to inspire, you'd include stories of courage in the face of adversity. Differences in purpose mean differences in content.

When I interviewed several authors and asked about their purposes for writing their books, each author volunteered without hesitating and shared a thoughtful response. What I noticed is that each author was motivated by something bigger and more important than simply having his or her name on a book. The purpose of performance coach and author Deirdre Van Nest's book *Fire Your Fear: How to Grow Your Business by Changing the Way You Think* is to help people make choices from a place of freedom, not fear. "I believe that when fear dictates our choices, it's difficult, if not impossible, for us to become the people we were created to be," Deirdre says. "I believe spreading this message is God's plan for my life. This helps me stay focused when I feel like throwing in the towel."

Be the Expert and Build Your Platform

One of the crucial characteristics of an indie author is confidence. I've always stressed to the authors with whom I've worked that confidence builds trust. If you're passionate about your topic—and you must be to have interest in writing a book about it—then own that passion and become the expert. We're in the Information Age, and to consumers, experts are the answer to staying informed. Readers are naturally curious, seeking the latest answers and solutions. Problem: I don't know how to landscape my yard. Solution: expert advice from an experienced landscaper.

Remember how you felt when you made your last book purchase. You were somehow convinced that the book in front of you offered something unique. You also believed that the author was capable of providing something interesting, enjoyable, and fulfilling in some way. When an author is an expert on a topic, readers feel assured. They open the book fully ready for a positive experience.

The more of an expert you prove yourself to be, the more value readers receive from your book.

The more of an expert you prove yourself to be, the more value readers receive from your book. However, you can't merely profess to be an expert. You'll need to back up claims of expertise with true and valuable messages that readers will find sincere and genuine. Readers will know if you're bluffing; you can't be an expert at face value. Many authors have tried and failed at proving "expertise."

Developing yourself into an expert is a time-consuming process, but it's definitely worth it if you intend to find, grow, and keep your readership. Start by observing your favorite experts, especially those in your book's genre. Study an expert to learn what makes her successful. What work did she put into becoming an authority on her subject? And most importantly, what's unique about her that keeps her audience intrigued? Become part of her online network. Follow and observe experts you respect through resources like Twitter and Facebook. Subscribe to newsletters offered, and if possible, attend a presentation, seminar, or workshop.

Buy and read books already written on your book's subject matter. Your knowledge is your product, and is the key to connecting with your audience and building a solid platform for your book. Excellent examples are out there of people already doing this well. Get out there, observe, and determine how to add something new and different to the expert pool.

"Platform" is a word that marketers throw around often. When you hear it, perhaps you cringe, thinking that you need to have a radio show or popular column in the *New York Times*. Think again. A platform simply describes the ways that you reach and attract your readership.[3] Your platform is how you (the author) make your calling, purpose, or expertise more visible. It should be a natural extension of your passion.

Many authors with whom I've worked do this by giving presentations, serving as expert speakers, or developing a strong and creative web presence. If you already have a readership, consider the work that went into growing that readership—that was platform building. Laying the groundwork for growing your platform is as simple as having readings of your work on a regular basis, or even sharing your work regularly through social media, which culti-

> **If you already have a readership, consider the work that went into growing that readership—that was platform building.**

vates your fan base and creates name recognition. Such grassroots marketing is all about a strategy, and it can help indie authors become well known and respected within their fields.

Teaching a course about your area of interest gives you a built-in audience, and this is true for fiction as well as nonfiction authors. Novelists often structure classes around writing techniques, but there are other areas fiction writers can become experts in, such as:

- A particular location
- A topic
- A time period
- A truth or phenomenon
- Universal human themes, such as redemption or compassion
- A particular time or phase in people's lives (coming of age, for example)
- The creative process

Places and opportunities to consider for teaching courses and holding workshops include the following:

- colleges, especially those with extension programs
- continuing education centers
- community and faith organizations
- local libraries or adult-education centers
- the workplace
- conferences

If public speaking and teaching are strengths of yours, create presentations based around your book's topic, or teach a class associated with it. If you'd like to become better at speaking, join a group like Toastmasters International, which helps thousands of entrepreneurs and authors become better speakers each year. Toastmasters, with more than 250,000 members worldwide, will improve your speaking techniques and also provide a strong networking environment. Toastmasters has a positive peer-counseling approach to speaking, and joining is cheaper than hiring a coach. If you're not able to get to a Toastmasters group or hire a coach, read *World Class Speaking: The Ultimate Guide to Presenting, Marketing and Profiting like a Champion* by Craig Valentine and Mitch Meyerson. Becoming a skilled speaker on your book's content will maximize your confidence, which only helps your book.

Where's the Beef? The Basics of a Book's Brand

A book is done well when it's an extension of the author's goals and conveys its purpose effectively. Your book's brand is your book's unique personality. If you understand your book's niche, it'll be easier to think about its brand (meaning its language, tone, format, and design). A book's brand can either be separate from or an extension of *your* personal brand. If you're using your book to propel yourself forward in a particular arena or industry, it's a good idea to have your book's brand reflect you.

Case Study:
The *New York Times* best seller *Skinny Bitch*.

What ingredients made this book an international hit? First off, it has an eye-raising title with two words that draw a reaction from most women: "skinny" and "bitch." Rory Freedman and Kim Barouin, the authors of the book, created quite the stir, especially because celebrities were seen touting the diet book, which promotes healthier eating habits. Their book is known for its straight talk and no-nonsense approach to dieting, which gave their diet book uniqueness and also served as their brand. On their website, you'll find this quote: "If you can't take one more day of self-loathing, you're ready to hear the truth: You cannot keep shoveling the same crap into your mouth every day and expect to lose weight." Whether you connect with the "skinny bitch" angle or not, they offer to solve a problem and appeal to the person seeking a straightforward weight-loss solution. The lesson learned is that angle, brand, and book content all tie together, and when they offer a solution or a compelling story, they attract readers.

Consider what comes to mind when you think of Suze Orman's personal finance books, the Chicken Soup for the Soul books, or a Stephen King novel. With the mere mention of Suze Orman, you can probably hear her confident cautioning about budgeting, saving, and contributing the maximum to your 401(k). Suze's books are about her expertise, and thus the book's personality is built around her personality. Chicken Soup for the Soul books evoke the warm and fuzzy feeling of wanting to curl up on the sofa with a bowl of chicken soup—these books have a brand separate from the authors, but a strong brand nonetheless. And Stephen King? His books are branded as page-turning chillers. Each of these examples has a clear "stamp" that readers automatically recognize. For most books, developing that stamp doesn't happen overnight, and as an author, you shouldn't feel that you have to work this out from the get go. However, if you've developed your platform and worked to expand your readership, establishing a known brand will come soon enough.

If your book could become the go-to book for "fill in the blank," or, as the author, you could become known for "fill in the blank," you've successfully created a strong book brand. One author I know is simply "The Cookie Lady." She's a nationally known blue-ribbon baker who has traveled the world with sweets in hand. Her book's brand is an extension of her "cookie lady" persona. The design, the text, and entire feel of the book is "grandmotherly" and warm. Another author I know is the "guy who knows secrets about the web," because his book teaches readers the unknowns of navigating the Internet. His book's brand is informative, authoritative, and content-focused.

The cool part about having a known brand is that you'll be stamped in the minds of your readers, hopefully permanently! Here are some important things to consider as you begin to flesh out your brand:

- List your eccentric qualities that strangers and those close to you comment on regularly. Work this into your book's style.
- Write down notable achievements that strengthen your credibility as the author.
- Define your personal style, and identify ways it enhances or stamps your book in a unique way.
- List sayings, mantras, or phrases that are uniquely yours. Use these in the book and especially in the promotion of the book.

As you think about your brand, don't get hung up on a catch phrase. Don't panic if you can't think of branding ideas right away. Again, your brand is your personality, and it'll come through in time. Your book's color scheme, visual aesthetic, and the unique tone of your writing all establish your brand. Several things often work together serendipitously to become your brand. Or perhaps you've always known your "shtick" and how you'll use it to stamp your book. Either way, go with your gut and never underestimate how to use your unique qualities to help readers remember you.

> **Your book's color scheme, visual aesthetic, and the unique tone of your writing all establish your brand.**

Discovering Your Audience

Don't rush to publish until you know your audience. A writer with a niche who knows his audience creates momentum more quickly than one who doesn't. "Turn your book inside and out and think about the unconventional people who would be interested," said author Suzanne Ruff. "The number-one strategy I use in promoting my book is targeting my audience. I think outside the bookstore. I've attracted unexpected audiences such as breast cancer patients, even though my book is for kidney disease patients." Indie authors understand that, ultimately, the book's publication isn't about them.

Readers want to be talked to, not talked at. Readers sink their teeth into a book when the author appears to truly know and understand their innermost needs and desires. Again, creating a product in today's market is about building relationships with your consumers. While it might be a tad unromantic to see your book as a "product," it's eye opening to know that your readers are yearning for what is ultimately important to them—your content. Your book should offer something original and stand apart from the competition. Knowing what makes your book unique comes from research and thoughtful evaluation of your book's market. One way to go about this is to create profiles of your customers. What do they read? Where do they shop? How often do they purchase books? Which websites do they frequent? The answers to these questions will help build your book's content, marketing plan, and sales strategy on a solid foundation that will reap long-term success.

Fiction writers may find answering questions about audience and niches more difficult than nonfiction writers. Over-analyzing a target market while writing can sometimes do more harm than good to your art. If you're a fiction writer, create a complete draft first. Once your story is all done, jot down keywords from your manuscript and use them to identify possible audiences. You may discover that with a

> **If you're a fiction writer, create a complete draft first. Once your story is all done, jot down keywords from your manuscript and use them to identify possible audiences.**

few small changes, your book will fit neatly into a specific genre you hadn't considered, such as young adult fiction. Once you've got a draft done, you may want to shape it toward a particular market segment, but don't let the market dictate and censor your initial creative output.

Whatever your book's genre, get out there and ask your readers what questions they want answered. Even if you don't find out the answers, knowing and addressing those questions puts you in a good spot with future readers. If you're a children's book author, you can "test" your audience by bringing your working manuscript into an actual classroom. In fact, one children's book author shared that she went into a classroom with a survey in hand for the students and their teacher to fill out at the end of her reading. She used their feedback to further strengthen the story. She measured from the survey which parts of her book were the strongest and built on that. Another author, whose book is about the loss of a pet, visited with several veterinarians, her primary market before publishing her book. Based on their feedback, she discovered veterinarians' preferences for explaining pet loss to younger children. She also learned the language they disliked and book features that would affect their buying decision. The author made critical changes to her storyline based on that feedback. If you believe your book is perfect for an MBA student, consider getting it reviewed by an MBA professor to see if your book is missing anything. If the feedback is good, take the opportunity to solicit a testimonial for your book.

Do Your Homework

Visit the section of the bookstore where you expect your book to be shelved. Note the look and feel of the books already shelved there, their prices, and the nature and style of the back-cover marketing copy. Note what you like and dislike. Ask the bookstore staff their opinions on the books that stand out. Booksellers are often willing to provide feedback and are a phenomenal resource.

Observe the books that catch the attention of consumers within that section. Which ones do they pull out and immediately put back, and which ones do they spend time leafing through? Buyers find some titles and covers more appealing—make mental notes along the way and jot down a few titles. If you're feeling brave, approach a buyer and ask for feedback on specific covers. Also, note the books that underwhelm buyers.

A major misconception authors have is that competition is non-existent. It's true that some books are one-of-a-kind, but most often that's not the case. I'm sure your approach and spin on your book's subject is trailblazing, but take the time to see what's already out there. After all, knowing what's already in the market will only empower your book to be truly pioneering. The questions below are things to consider as you research competing titles. In the business world, this is known as a competitive analysis. Your answers will not only help strengthen your vision, but will be valuable in marketing your book, because you'll know your audience better.

1. What is the demand for your book's category?
2. Who are competitive authors? Are they well known? Would they write a testimonial for you if you approached them?
3. What's the average retail price for the hardcovers, paperbacks, and e-books in your genre?
4. What's the ratio of paperbacks to hardcovers in your genre? What does this say about the audience and your choice for publishing your book as a paperback or hardcover?
5. How successful are e-books in your book's genre? Do electronic sales outpace paper sales, or is it the other way around? What does this say about where to focus your efforts?
6. What do the books in your genre look like? Are they printed in color or in black and white? Do they contain photographs and images throughout? Are there photographs inserted in the middle?
7. What are the keywords in the title, subtitle, and back-cover copy? What words jump out when you look at the book front to back?
8. Are the books on the shelf old or new? What are the differences between books published recently and those published a while ago?

9. What special features do you notice in competitive books? Do they have cover treatments, like raised lettering and embellished graphics? Is there a particular binding that you notice (e.g., hardcover binding)?
10. Who are the reviewers? What are the themes in the testimonials?
11. In your opinion, what makes competing books more appealing to you as a consumer?

As you answer these questions, you'll expand your vision. The trick is to avoid modeling your book after the competition. Your unique spin and take on the competition is the foundation you need to build on. One example of a unique spin is from an author I've worked with who is a sports history buff. Since "sports" is such a popular genre, he decided against writing a general history of his favorite teams. Instead, he took a nostalgic look at teams that moved on, either to other states or stadiums. His books focus on a snapshot of a specific period near and dear to the hearts of fans who reminisce about the "good old days." His sales continue to climb, despite the "advice" he got that no one would buy his books.

Budgeting Basics

Take the time to consider the expenses you'll incur while publishing your book *before* you draft a publishing and marketing plan. This will put you miles ahead of the average indie author. Thinking about your book financially shows where you've got flexibility in the publishing process and where you don't, and it will it help you do the following:

1. Ensure you have the funds to take on publishing and that you've received true cost estimates for the entire book process from your publishing consultants or hired vendors.
2. Understand the specifics of what services you'll need to employ in producing your book.
3. Avoid being caught off guard as bills come in.

Another benefit of the many publishing options out there is that there's something for every budget. The key to choosing the best option for you is being clear about the reality of what you can afford. As author Colleen Baldrica said, "Really look at self-publishing financially. Not every book is going to make it. If you can't afford to gamble, don't do it. Worrying about the finances every step will take the joy out of the process." Collecting quotes and estimates on services you'll need is the absolute best way to know how to budget and measure your investment.

To get a good working estimate, list every service or product you'll need to produce your book. Do you need an editor? (I always insist that every author, experienced or not, have a professional editor look at his or her work.) Do you have solutions for distributing your book? Will you employ a book publicist to help with marketing? Will you print postcards, bookmarks, business cards, and sell sheets? Will you invest in a website? What about an e-book? The people and places you contact for estimates should be able to share itemized costs and payment timeframes.

If service providers fail to communicate these factors or show the slightest apprehension to share them, consider it a sign. However, some service costs are difficult to determine until all the details are figured out. For instance, you may opt for two, three, or several rounds of edits. Also, quotes given by designers and printers won't be exact if your page count is not final. However, you should be able to get a ballpark figure to help you anticipate the probable expenses.

Don't base your publishing decisions on what you currently have or don't have in the bank. You'll have an easier time and more success focusing realistically on the true costs of each service item. Once you look at the costs of producing your book, take the time to set a sales goal of how many books you intend to sell in the first year. You'll reach this esti- mate by guessing the number of read- ers you expect to pick up your book per month, based on your marketing efforts. Here's where your marketing plan comes in handy. For example, if you intend to engage in five promotional or selling

> **Once you look at the costs of producing your book, take the time to set a sales goal of how many books you intend to sell in the first year.**

opportunities per month, figure you'll sell on average twenty to fifty books at each event. That works out to be 1,200 to 3,000 copies by the year's end. You'll need to factor into your sales figures bookstore dis- counts, promotional sale discounts, and bulk sale discounts. Consider setting your book production efforts up as a limited liability com- pany (LLC). Derek Wolden, financial planner and successful author of a how-to book, advised, "Set up your own company, because it allows for a lot of tax breaks that will save you money. You can recoup costs if you're business savvy before you even start talking about publishing."

Your Indie Author Publishing Checklist

Getting Started: Organization and Planning

☐ Write your book and self edit

☐ Start interviewing mentoring presses (DIY authors interview editors, book designers, and proofreaders)

☐ Create a publishing plan to guide your publishing journey

☐ Visit your favorite bookstore to scope out the competition

☐ Brainstorm your title and subtitle. Poll your friends and colleagues. Once you've narrowed it down, check to see if they're taken on www.booksinprint.com and www.amazon.com

☐ Begin collecting or making note of books that have an appealing design. Scope out the competition's design

☐ While looking at competing titles, research prices to get a sense of reasonable price options for your book

☐ Join IBPA (Independent Book Publishers Association) and SPAN (The Small Publisher's Association of North America)

☐ As you work through the manuscript, pull out excerpts that would make good standalone articles, blog posts, and good content for your marketing materials

☐ Consider setting up a business license (call your county Business License Division for details). With the license, you might want to open a business checking account for all business transactions related to your book

(continued)

☐ Create a Twitter account for your book

☐ Create a Facebook Fan Page for your book

☐ Create a LinkedIn account, and add "author" to your profile

☐ Subscribe to, like, and follow books of similar content on Facebook, LinkedIn, and Twitter

☐ Start researching and following blogs of similar content, blogs by other indie authors, and blogs about self-publishing

☐ Sign up for Google alerts

☐ Sign up for Google Analytics and add to website once launched

Book Building: Preparing for Publication

☐ Secure your ISBN

☐ Secure your Library of Congress Control Number

☐ Submit book info to Bowker's Books in Print

☐ Begin working with your book editor

☐ Review changes when they're done. The editing and revisions process takes on average four to six weeks

☐ Start building your list of important contacts including friends, family, colleagues, media, organizations, authors, and events coordinators

☐ Select your book designer

(continued)

☐ Begin working with designer to craft your book's promotional materials (sell sheet, postcard, business card, and bookmark)

☐ Create your back cover or dust jacket flap copy

☐ Put together your list of reviewers for back-of-the-book testimonials or "blurbs." Think about authors and other "key influencers" in your subject area

☐ Purchase a domain name for your book's website

☐ Begin the design process, which takes on average four weeks.

In the meantime...

☐ Confirm book specifications (page count, trim size, paperback/hardcover, and other details)

☐ Collect printer quotes

☐ Select a website vendor

☐ Write website content and secure photos for website pages

☐ Send book proof to proofreader

☐ Send 1st book proof files to galley printer (if applicable)

☐ Mail galleys to book reviewers and endorsers

☐ Send final corrections from proofreader to designer

☐ Send pre-publication endorsements and reviews to designer

☐ Approve final book proof from designer

☐ Send final book files to book printer

(continued)

☐ Determine if your book is going to bookstores. If so, do the following:

   ☐ Submit book information to Ingram Book Company

   ☐ Submit book information to Baker & Taylor

Book Launch: Marketing and Promotion

☐ Brainstorm and target at least three nontraditional sales opportunities

☐ Research book clubs that might be a fit for your title at Literary Marketplace or www.booksonline.com. Contact the acquisitions editor of the good candidates, pitch them, and offer to e-mail sample chapters or send a galley when done

☐ Organize a blog tour by contacting bloggers and offering to post a guest blog

☐ Invest an hour a day updating your book's page on Facebook, networking on Twitter, and commenting on blogs targeted to your audience

☐ Create op-eds and articles around the topic of your book

☐ Research and plan to have a table at conferences, tradeshows, festivals, and fairs

☐ Visit Lions clubs, rotary clubs, and networking groups, and schedule speaking opportunities to promote your book

THE LAST WORD

- Create a publishing plan around your mission statement to keep yourself grounded through the publishing process.
- Use your personality, knowledge, unique life experiences, and passion to build and grow your platform and brand to become the known expert on your book's subject matter.
- Position your book to outshine the competition by doing your research and knowing what the competition offers. Use that knowledge to position and shape your book as uniquely as possible.
- Factor the real costs of publishing your book with the highest quality, not what you hope it will cost, or how much money you have to spend. Like everything else, you get what you pay for.
- Examine and come to understand your audience prior to making the leap. Your choices in publishing should be influenced by how your audience might be best reached.

Indie Author Wisdom

"Believe in yourself, your book, and never give up!"

~Gregg Proteaux, author of *Attitudes at Every Altitude*

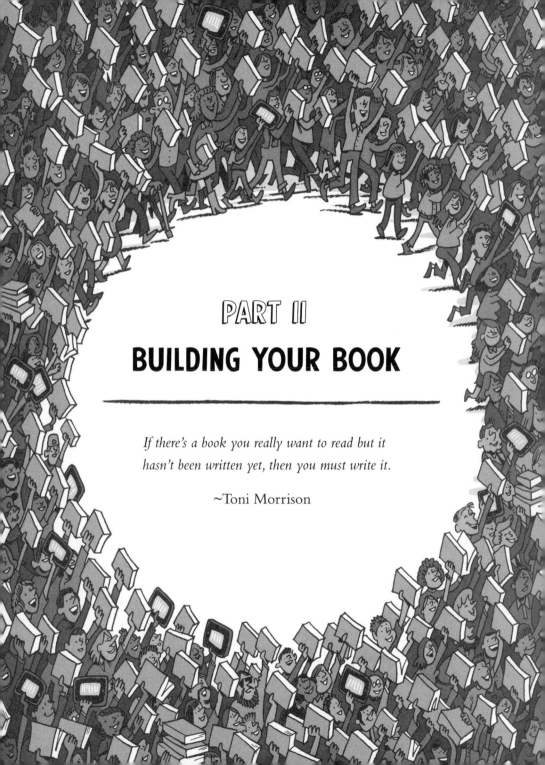

PART II
BUILDING YOUR BOOK

If there's a book you really want to read but it hasn't been written yet, then you must write it.

~Toni Morrison

The ABCs of Writing for Publication

There are several good books on writing, and no doubt, you've read half of them. My personal favorites are William Zinsser's *On Writing Well* and the *Portable MFA in Creative Writing* by the New York Writer's Workshop. The book you're holding now isn't a book on writing, but I've got some important pointers to share before moving onto the next phase of the process. By the time I meet most authors, their books are already written, and they think they're ready for editing; some are, but some are definitely not, and it's always painful when I have to send them back to the keyboard. Sure, a good editor will help perfect what has been written. Editors, however, are not usually in the business of rewriting an entire work. If you don't do your part to get the manuscript in "ready" form when it reaches the editor, it'll cost you!

Luckily, there are steps to take to prevent a high editing bill and to ensure quality. If you're self-publishing, you don't want your book to fall into that category of "just okay." A "just okay" book diminishes your effort and defeats its chances of reaping the same respect as a traditionally published book. Sharpen your skills. Join a writer's group, check out writing workshops, or take a creative writing class. And before the pen hits the paper, ask yourself: *Who, What, Why,* and *How.*

Getting to the Good Stuff: Your Beginning, Middle, and End

Another little-acknowledged thing to keep in mind is that every book must have three elements: a beginning, middle, and end. Many authors jump right into writing, and that's okay, but once you start crafting a book, you must give thought to the book's structure. You're moving readers in a direction whether you're writing fiction or nonfiction, and your job as a writer is to be in control of the direction they take. You control that direction with the content, the arrangement of chapters, and by reminding readers of goals along the way. You don't have to write in order; often the beginning is the last thing finalized. Just make sure the beginning goes in the front, and the end goes in the back.

The Key Questions Your Book Must Answer

- Who are you writing to and why?
- What important problem are you solving?
- What makes you qualified to write this book?
- Why do people need your solution?
- How is your solution different from others addressing the same problem?

Starting with the beginning of your book, you want to draw your readers in and provide a reason to keep them turning the page. Whether you're writing fiction or nonfiction, your readers are used to a fast-paced world that grabs their attention immediately. For fiction, this specifically means introducing the characters and conflict in the story's opening. One tip is to drop readers right into the action and not bore them with complex details that should come later in the manuscript (if ever). Another tip is to read *The First Five Pages* by Noah Lukeman, an excellent book for writers (especially fiction writers) on how to avoid common mistakes in your story's opening. This book gives valuable insight on ways to create a powerful beginning.

For nonfiction, immediately introduce the problem or identify the need that your book addresses. Don't beat around the bush or build up to it. Keep in mind that an interested buyer only spends a few moments at the bookstore (or online) leafing through the beginning pages before determining quickly if it's worth their time and money. One way to snag their attention is by immediately raising an urgent question in their minds—and promise that you'll explore it, and provide solutions.

Your book's middle provides the nuts and bolts of your content. It's where your book proves its case and delivers on its promise—where your readers sink their teeth in and have the bulk of their questions answered. The Three Es are also important in the middle of your book. You need to enlighten, empower, and engage in order to provide a good read for your audience.

Your ending is important; it ties everything together and perhaps even challenges your reader to take action. A mistake that some authors make, especially fiction writers, is continuing the story beyond its ending. A good writer knows when to stop. A little book titled *Gone with the Wind* by Margaret Mitchell caught flak from readers who needed to know what happened to Scarlett O'Hara after Rhett Butler's infamous "Frankly my dear, I don't give a damn." Today, most Margaret Mitchell fans appreciate that *Gone with the Wind* didn't go on forever, as it probably could have. In fact, an intensely marketed authorized sequel was a disaster because it couldn't live up to the readers' visions and paled in comparison to Mitchell's version. Mitchell left room for readers to imagine their own endings, and she wisely followed the age-old adage, "Leave them wanting more."

Despite what you might think, it's okay to leave some ends untied, especially if you don't have all the answers. Occasional and intentional open-endedness is perceived by readers as honest and will challenge them to contemplate their own best answers. For fiction writers, creating an ending that emotionally connects with the reader is all you need. However, there's a big difference between ending and simply stopping. Your readers need to feel catharsis. They need to feel like you've taken them on a worthwhile journey. When Rhett finally walks out on Scarlett, we know he won't be coming back. And we don't blame him. In nonfiction, it's perfectly acceptable to simply end on your long-term outlook for your book's subject.

> **Occasional and intentional open-endedness is perceived by readers as honest and will challenge them to contemplate their own best answers.**

Staying Away from Trends

As a writer, you've probably looked at a book on the best seller list and felt you could do a much better job. Or like me, thought, *Why didn't I think of that!* But if you're perusing the best sellers aisle at your local bookstore for ideas, my advice is to think again. Conforming to some current writing trend—through topic or even style—probably won't get your book there, and by the time you're done with your manuscript, the trend that inspired you will probably be over.

And a Few Extra Notes About Writing Fiction

If you were in a creative writing program, here's the advice your Fiction 101 instructor would give about developing the concept for your first draft:

1. **A good place to begin fiction writing is from your own experience.** Your life is often the best place to begin your writing. This doesn't mean that your book should necessarily be an autobiography or personal memoir, but writing about what you know lends authenticity and complexity to themes, characters, setting, and your voice. Oftentimes, small moments in our lives represent a larger truth or "ah ha" moment.

2. **Start with a story you were told by someone else.** Have you ever heard a story and instantly felt it was compelling material for a book? The next time you hear a provocative story, consider how you'd present it if you

had to write it. How would you capture the storyteller's voice? What would you want readers to take away from your version of this story?

3. **Forget the rules!** Most writing coaches and MFA instructors would tell you to write from your soul, get the story down on paper (or on the screen), and don't think about the "rules of writing" while you're in the zone.

4. **Okay, now look at the rules.** Once your draft is complete, think about the rules. They're there for a reason.

5. **Avoid clichés, stereotypes, and one-dimensional characters.** Authenticity is important in fiction writing. Books that connect with readers are the ones readers believe. Whatever your audience or genre, your characters should be multidimensional, and readers should want to know more about them. Remember the goal: bring your readers into the world of your story.

6. **Be prepared to be scared to death.** Writing is hard. You might hear voices (your own or even others) that question your writing ability and even question why anyone would want to read your book in the first place. Ignore these voices and know that every writer goes through this. In the words of Ralph Waldo Emerson, "Always do what you are afraid to do."

Choosing the Right Title for Your Book

We all know that, despite the old adage, books are judged by their covers. In fact, books are judged by their covers *and* by their titles. Choosing a riveting title for your book is one of the most important decisions you will make. I don't believe there's a single magic title for any one book whose rejection destines your book for failure. Every book has several possible choices, and the best fit will be the title that most represents your book's mission and succinctly conveys your book's promise. But some titles are better than others. F. Scott Fitzgerald was torn between calling his masterpiece *Among the Ash-Heaps and Millionaires* or *The Great Gatsby*. The story is a classic regardless of the title, but doesn't *The Great Gatsby* sound like a more inviting, enjoyable read? It's catchy, memorable, and not easily confused with something else.

For nonfiction, I suggest a short, captivating title of six words or less, followed by a subtitle that explains what readers will discover in your book. A good example is Bob Adams's *Streetwise Complete Business Plan: Writing a Business Plan Has Never Been Easier!* Or take a look at *Help! For Writers: 210 Solutions to the Problems Every Writer Faces* by Roy Peter Clark. Both titles are succinct and contain the books' subjects: business plans and writers. The subtitles tell the reader what they will get from these books. There's no guesswork involved. **When brainstorming titles:**

1. Start with a list of possible titles.
2. Choose a main title of six words or less. *Catcher in the Rye; Because of Winn Dixie; A Whole New Mind; The Kid Stays in the Picture; The House on Mango Street; A Tree Grows in Brooklyn.*
3. Include the subject of your book: *The Joy of Cooking; The Seven Habits of Highly Successful People; The Marriage Plot.*

4. Create a subtitle that informs readers what they will get from your book title: *Blink: The Power of Thinking Without Thinking; Freakonomics: A Rogue Economist Explores the Hidden Side of Everything; Into Thin Air: A Personal Account of the Mt. Everest Disaster.*

5. For fiction, think of words or phrases that are catchy and perhaps mysterious: *One Flew Over the Cuckoo's Nest; The Time Traveler's Wife; The Secret Life of Bees; The Wind Through the Keyhole.*

6. Choose words that relate closely to the crux of the story that aren't obvious: *To Kill a Mockingbird; The Sweet Science; The Color Purple; A River Runs Through It; Bang the Drum Slowly.*

7. Go for rhythm—rhythm makes a title memorable: *Always Outnumbered, Always Outgunned; What to Expect When You're Expecting; I Know Why the Caged Bird Sings; Murder on the Orient Express; Friday Night Lights.*

8. Try juxtaposing contrasting words or ideas: *Smart Women, Foolish Choices; Swim With the Sharks Without Getting Eaten Alive; Reading Lolita in Tehran; The Lovely Bones; Chicken Soup for the Soul.*

9. Select the short, easy-to-remember title over a complex title that would require an explanation: *The Not-So-Big House; Mommie Dearest; Paradise Lost; Diary of a Wimpy Kid; The One Minute Manager; The Four Hour Work Week; Helter Skelter*

10. Ask others for their thoughts about potential titles.

Common Writing Mistakes When Preparing a Manuscript for Publication

Some writers may come across as amateurs due to small, preventable mistakes. **Here's a quick list of what I see most often:**

1. **Wordiness**: In an effort to wow the reader, authors do the opposite by overusing words and long phrases that could easily be pared down. For example, change "in the field of marketing" to "marketing," and change "have a tendency to" to "tend to." The accomplice to wordiness is redundancy. All writers write useless sentences, paragraphs, and sometimes entire chapters. Seek and destroy bloat. Those deadbeat words cost you money! Editing, design, proofreading, printing, and shipping are priced based on word count, page count, and weight. Focus on *that* when you're loathe to streamline. To save time and money during the publishing process, study a book such as *Copyediting: A Practical Guide* by Karen Judd, and apply those principles to your manuscript,

2. **Jargon**: In most books meant for general readers, everyday language beats jargon, and editors and readers prefer it. Don't use words that you wouldn't use in normal conversation. Again, your job is to connect with your audience on an emotional level, draw them in, and keep them wanting more. Jargon breaks all of those rules. If you wouldn't say it in real life, reword or delete it all together.

3. **Inconsistencies**: If your book is written in past tense, keep it that way through the whole book unless readers can determine the reason for a switch (a chapter that takes place in a different time, for example). Similarly, if your book is written in first person, the narration shouldn't arbitrarily switch to third person. If you write "website" without a hyphen or space, don't later use "web site" or "web-site." Even something as simple as indicating percentage—whether by the word or symbol—should be kept consistent. Continuity is part of consistency. If the book opens in the cold of winter, it remains winter, until you indicate otherwise. This means your characters' actions, descriptions, and dialogue must make sense in a winter setting, so no beach parties or sundresses.

Search for these problems and others before you show it to anyone else. After the long lonely slog of writing a draft, you'll have a strong desire to show it around, but do yourself a favor and wait. Put it down for a while, at least a few weeks, so that you can review it with fresh eyes. While your draft is resting, read up on editing to prepare yourself. Then go through your manuscript with as much detachment as possible, and make the cuts and changes that must be made. Do this before you show it to anyone, including your dearest loved ones and especially, your editor.

You don't want your editor to be the first person to read your manuscript in its raw entirety. Do as much as you possibly can on your own first. Think of it like "cleaning for the cleaning lady." If you pay a cleaning lady to spend a few hours in your home and you've got junk scattered everywhere and dishes in the sink, she will be too busy tidying up the surface clutter to tackle the deep cleaning you really need. If you don't much care about the quality of your manuscript, your editor won't care much either. And an editor can always tell how much you care.

In the end, bringing an editorial eye to your work is important to your manuscript's quality as well as your pocketbook. **Here's a quick checklist of basic things that will reduce your editing and proofreading costs**[4]:

- ☐ Check all spelling, hyphens, capitals, numbers, and important names and terms.
- ☐ Identify organizational problems and make a note of them to help your editor.
- ☐ Shorten long sentences.
- ☐ Check that subjects and verbs agree.
- ☐ Make sure your book's purpose is clear to your reader.
- ☐ Search for *there are* and rewrite these sentences.
- ☐ Search for *and*. Consider breaking these sentences into two sentences.
- ☐ Search for *just, very, really*, and *actually*, and remove.
- ☐ Consistently use either "for example" or "e.g."
- ☐ Consistently use either in "other words" or "i.e."
- ☐ Search periods and commas following quotation marks.
- ☐ Search for two spaces after periods, question marks, and exclamation marks and replace with a single space.

☐ Use a grammar checker to find passive voice sentences, and rewrite in active voice.

☐ Check capitalization in all chapter and section titles.

☐ Cut text that doesn't add to or serve your book.

☐ Proofread everything that you send out or have a trusted friend or family member proofread for you. Fresh eyes help!

Though the writing process is uncertain, there are two things you can be sure of: You'll face missteps along the way, and self-editing helps eradicate mistakes. All of this is normal and natural, even for the professionals who have been writing for decades. In Susan Bell's *The Artful Edit,* she describes F. Scott Fitzgerald's correspondence with his editor, Max Perkins. You'd take comfort in seeing the extent of what Fitzgerald's manuscripts had to go through before they were made final! The next time you question yourself and you're anxious in the face of writing and revising, also think of something Maya Angelou says in her book *Letter to My Daughter.* Describing her anxiety as she approaches writing each new masterpiece, she says, "When I decide to write anything, I get caught up in my insecurity despite the prior accolades. I think, *uh, uh, now they will know I am a charlatan that I really cannot write and write really well.* I am almost undone, then I pull out a new yellow pad and as I approach the clean page, I think of how blessed I am." I love this quote because it reminds us that self-doubt is something we all go through and that it's okay.

- Make sure your book has a beginning, middle, and end.
- Stay away from writing about what is trendy at the moment or what you think will "sell." Instead, tap into your passion and write from your "reader place."
- Have fun during the writing process. After all, your book is your creation. Take your time and don't forget to take breaks!
- Choose a title that creates a picture in your reader's mind of the value they will discover in your book.
- Save time and money by avoiding common writing mistakes through self-editing. Make sure your book's purpose is clear along the way.

Indie Author Wisdom

"Take the leap of faith if you believe in your story. There will never be 'a perfect time' to tackle the endeavor. Your kids may be young, you may be struggling at work, and you may feel like you have zero time to get anything done (much less writing). But if you have the determination and are willing to put yourself out there, you will not regret it."

~Susie Bazil, award-winning author of The Sick Bug series

Chapter 5

The Editorial Process

If you've ever had your writing edited, you know how intimidating it feels. One author compared editing with a trip to the dentist. As a writer myself, I am accustomed to all the insecurities that go along with it. I agree that having someone scrutinize your work is tough, but an editor is absolutely needed. Besides, your editor is on your side and wants your book to be as good as possible. As author Deirdre Van Nest puts it:

> *The ability to get my thoughts out in a cohesive manner that would make sense to others was most important to me. That's where my editor helped immensely. It would have been hard to do that alone. She was great at helping me figure out the right direction for my book and the overall message. My book started in one direction and then took another.*

Deirdre's goal of wanting her thoughts conveyed cohesively is the precise reason good editors are truly extraordinary—it is their job to make good writing even better. Still, I meet authors who question the need for editing and see it as a place to shave dollars. Deciding not to hire a professional editor is a grave mistake. One author (let's call her Bonnie), recently discovered this. Bonnie felt that her network of family and close friends, all of whom have exceptional credentials, were good enough editors for her book. She decided against spending additional dollars to hire a professional editor, believing that a proofread was all her book needed. Several problems occurred as a result, including a number of mistakes found by the proofreader that her book designer had to correct. Too many corrections in the book design phase introduced more errors, and consequently, Bonnie spent more time and money to make her manuscript clean. The money Bonnie saved in not hiring an editor she spent in the design phase. She also spent countless hours going through the manuscript repeatedly, only to find more mistakes. Avoid Bonnie's experience by hiring a professional editor who'll help eliminate your manuscript's trouble spots.

A common misconception is that editing is the same as proofreading. This is not true. Proofreading is the final glossing of the fully-edited manuscript prior to publication. Editing is the process of a professional editor reading a manuscript, evaluating and interpreting it for grammar, syntax, clarity, focus, organization, and style. An editor recommends changes, additions, and deletions based on his or her evaluation and interpretation. Editors are well acquainted with language and identify ambiguity (the possibility of one or more reasonable interpretations of the same word, phrase, or sentence), inconsistency, and errors in spelling, punctuation, and grammar. Editors also follow standards in writing according to style guides, which are trusted references that make consistent recommendations about all elements of style and grammar. The standard style guide for most nontechnical publishers is *The Chicago Manual of Style.* If your book is intended for a general audience, hire an editor who knows *The Chicago Manual of Style* and will refer to it while editing your book. Also, make sure that your editor is experienced, and request samples of other books he or she has edited.

My philosophy is that the final word rests with the author, so I consider editors' marks suggestions, not demands. But they are well-reasoned, well-founded suggestions, and all suggestions from experienced editors are worth considering. Editors have years of experience working with manuscripts. They anticipate how readers are likely to react to your writing. Work with your editor to understand his or her suggestions; never reject a change without understanding the editor's intention. A copyeditor for more than ten years with Editorial Inspirations, April Michelle Davis advises authors: "Be open and willing to discuss the manuscript. Authors and editors need to work as a team, especially because they're both striving for the same goal."

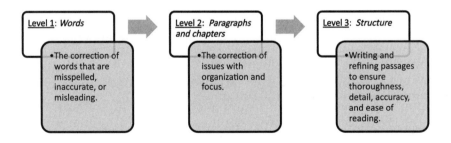

The Three Levels of Editing

One of the most important contributions editors make is their unbiased judgment about whether a reader will fully understand your points. "Many beginning authors believe their writing is better than it is," says Davis. "They believe they have no need for editors because their writing is perfect already."

When your manuscript comes back from your editor, you have the opportunity to accept or reject the editor's suggestions, to otherwise address the editor's questions, and to revise. Questions from an editor about the manuscript and disagreements about style between editor and author are not unusual and don't always signal a significant problem. Questions and disagreements are a normal part of writing and revising, and they typically lead to improvements. If your editor asks questions and challenges some of your points, he or she is, in fact, doing his or her job. Any questions an editor has about your manuscript are ones your readers will probably have too. Your editor should challenge you to think about things that might not have occurred to you while writing. His or her job is to reveal areas that need development or enhancement. This is what you're paying your editor to do. So don't take it personally if you're challenged to rewrite some aspects of your work. Think of your book like a boat that you'll be sailing across the ocean. An editor rigorously checks for cracks and makes sure it's seaworthy. When you're heading into those big waves later on, you'll thank (or curse!) your editor's work.

When edits come back to you, weigh the editor's suggestions, your readers' expectations, and your own judgment before accepting or rejecting a change. It's always reasonable, and recommended, to ask why your editor has made a suggestion. If you dislike an edit, give your editor a chance to explain his or her reasoning. As you navigate through the writing and editing process, remember that every masterpiece can stand one more round of editing and revising. Your book is no different. The most unforgettable compliment that your book may receive is that it is well written, which means high-quality editing was involved.

Here's a checklist of reasonable expectations. Your copyeditor should do the following:

- ☐ Make suggestions for rewriting where your meaning is unclear and sentences are awkward.
- ☐ Ensure correct punctuation and grammar as described in *The Chicago Manual of Style* or other appropriate style guide.
- ☐ Highlight inconsistencies in spelling, capitalization, hyphenation, and the use of numbers and abbreviations.
- ☐ Prepare a detailed style sheet.
- ☐ Query possible errors or ambiguous places in the manuscript.
- ☐ Alert the author to libel, permissions problems, copyright violations, and incorrect or missing citations.
- ☐ Verify the spelling of names, dates, and proper nouns.
- ☐ Verify all cross-references and headings.
- ☐ Review artwork, paying particular attention to captions.

When it comes to your manuscript, your voice should be distinctively yours. After all, self-publishing offers the benefit of complete control over your unique voice. While I hope you'll trust your editor's suggestions in the end, no one knows your book better than you. If your editor attempts to substitute your voice for his or her style, you'd be right to object. Plenty of editors are willing to help you make needed improvements without completely altering your manuscript beyond recognition. Also, if your editor isn't interested in your book's success, don't keep him or her around. Editors are not perfect and do make mistakes. But as a general species, editors love books, enjoy words, care about writers, and will help raise a manuscript to its best. April Michelle Davis explained, "Any book that conveys what the author wants to convey in a clear, concise, and well thought-out manner is considered well edited."

An Editor's Dream Client: Organizing and Preparing Your Book for Editing

Once your book is ready for your editor, don't send your manuscript in pieces. Provide it all in one complete document. Think through all the components of your manuscript thoroughly, such as the book text, the front matter (which goes in the front of your book), and the back matter (which follows your book content). Here's my rundown of components to create and have edited in addition to your manuscript (you may not have all of these components in your manuscript):

Copyright Page

The copyright is most often on the back of the title page. You could list yourself or create your own publishing imprint if you haven't hired a publisher. If you have hired a publisher, they should provide the content for this page. The copyright page includes an address, phone

Sample Style Sheet

Reference Sources

Chicago Manual of Style, 16th edition

Merriam-Webster's Collegiate Dictionary, 11th edition

Style Notes

- Generally capitalize the second element in a hyphenated word in a title/header.
- The CMS general rule is to spell out whole numbers from one to one hundred, round numbers, and any number beginning a sentence.
- Percentages are always given in numerals. In most humanistic work, the word "percent" is used rather than the % symbol.
- Italicize the titles of books, magazines, and newspapers.
- When mentioning a town or city and the state in which it is located, place a comma after the name of the state. E.g., "The weather of Minneapolis, Minnesota, is unpredictable."
- Lowercase roles or titles unless they function as part of a person's name. E.g., "Sara is the executive editor. Meet Executive Editor Walker."
- Place a comma after "i.e." and "e.g."
- Use curly (aka smart) quotes.

(continued)

- The prefixes pre, super, multi, and non usually don't take hyphens (see CMS 7.85 for exceptions).
- Make quotations of forty-five words or more into indented, block quotations.

Word List

- aha
- already-growing (adj. before a noun)
- already-perfect (adj. before a noun)
- already-strong (adj. before a noun)

  ———

- back-cover (adj. before a noun)
- backup
- best seller(s)
- best-selling (adj. before a noun)
- break-even (adj.)
- brick-and-mortar (adj. before a noun)

  ———

- cliché
- coffee-table

- e-mail
- e-zines

  ———

- goal oriented (adj. after a noun)
- guidebooks

  ———

- ill prepared (adj. after a noun)

  ———

- little-known (adj. before a noun)
- million-dollar (adj. before a noun)
- multidimensional
- nonexistent

  ———

- nonfiction
- nonprofit
- nonstop

(continued)

- nontraditional
- number-one (adj. before a noun)

  _____

- ongoing

  _____

- postcard
- precut
- predetermined
- prepublication

  _____

- roller-coaster (adj. before a noun)

  _____

- sales testing
- self-publishing

- short stories
- side-sewn (adj. before a noun)
- straightforward
- superclear

  _____

- test-drive
- Three Es (no apostrophe)

  _____

- web
- website
- well attended (adj. after a noun)
- well received (adj. after a noun)

number, and website for book ordering. Many copyright pages have what's called an impression line, which is a row of numbers that indicates the year the book was printed and the number of printings the book has had. I've included a sample copyright page in appendix C.

Acknowledgments

As you're writing, keep a list of the people who inspired you to write, who helped shape your book, and who supported you throughout the self-publishing process. The acknowledgements section is an appropriate place to credit your family, friends, editor(s), book designer, website designer, proofreader, coaches, and even organizations that helped or served as a resource. Giving credit is always an appreciated gesture and adds a nice touch. It can go in the beginning or at the end of your book.

Dedication

Most books are dedicated to a person, a philosophy, or group of people. Dedications are personal and can be connected to your book's content or not. Maybe it's dedicated to the memory of a loved one no longer living, to your spouse and children, or to everyone who wears the color blue—it's up to you. A health and fitness book on my desk entitled *Lose It!* is dedicated to "Everyone who is out there losing it!" Be succinct; it's a valentine, not a love letter.

Table of Contents

Make a list of your chapter titles, heading names, and other components you want highlighted in the table of contents. Don't worry about page numbers; you won't know those until the book is formatted by your book designer who will put the correct page numbers in for you. The structure and organization of your book is important at this stage, so a well-organized and final table of contents will significantly assist your editor and designer.

Foreword and Preface

Following your table of contents, some books have either a foreword (not to be confused with "forward") or a preface. It's rare that books have both. Forewords are written by someone who is not the author, most often a well-known or notable person who appeals to your book's audience. A foreword's purpose is to rally readers and inspire confidence in the book. If you don't have a heavy-hitter lined up to write your foreword, it's no big deal. In such a case, a preface serves the same purpose. A preface is similar to a foreword but is written by the author and addressed to the reader. A preface is your brief introduction to the book and is typically around 250 to 500 words in length. Prefaces are often conversational essays that describe how the book came to development, what the author's background is, or what readers will gain from the book.

Prologue

Similar to a preface, a prologue is a short introduction, typically found in fiction and is usually part of the fictional narrative. A prologue is set apart from the plot, most often by a specific amount of time. It sets the stage for the story by providing important background information. Use a prologue to dangle the hook, but keep it short. A prologue should be a teaser, not a full chapter.

Introduction

The introduction is a comprehensive overview of your book's purpose, its key messages, and the tools it will present to readers. A good introduction captures the reader right away and prompts immediate immersion into the book. Address your audience at once and steer clear of overwhelming the introduction with the meat of the main manuscript. Stick to the large-scale scope and leave the micro stuff for the chapter content.

Conclusion

A conclusion is completely optional. If you find that the last chapter of your book isn't necessarily how you want it to end, a conclusion might be the way to wrap everything up and leave the readers feeling the way you intend them to feel. Nonfiction books typically end positively with the author's "bottom-line" front and center. Imagine you're the captain of your book, and the conclusion is your final send-off speech. Steer clear of repeating too much of what's already been said, and structure the conclusion around a narrative that personally resonates with readers.

Epilogue

Fiction authors often write epilogues as a way to conclude a story. Though not required, epilogues tend to finalize scenes, wrap up a story's loose ends, or set up a sequel. Epilogues are often written apart from the rest of the plot and should be short and sweet.

Resources and Appendices

Readers will find value in a nonfiction book equipped with a comprehensive and current resource section that supplements the content. This section should include books, websites, organizations, and publications that complement or expand upon the book's content. Almost every nonfiction book lends itself well to a thoughtful resources section. A simple online search will produce several ideas for appropriate books, websites, and groups to include. Appendices are sections that include material too complex to have in the main text, such as sample documents or tables. It's also used to segment the various components of back matter. (See Appendices in this book for examples.)

Glossary

A glossary is needed only if your book introduces several uncommon industry- or trade-related terms that your audience might not be familiar with. Some children's books use glossaries to build vocabulary words. In fiction, a glossary clarifies the definition of language used intermittently that might be from another language or from a different time period.

Here's my quick checklist for organizing and preparing your manuscript:

- ☐ Front matter (all the pages before the first page of the text): table of contents, dedication page, acknowledgements page, foreword or preface, prologue, and title page.
- ☐ Final version of the manuscript typed in Times New Roman, 12-point font and double spaced.

- ☐ All text on one file and supplied on a CD or flash drive (i.e., don't save each chapter as a single file).
- ☐ Book's summary in one hundred fifty words or less.
- ☐ Author biography.
- ☐ Back matter (all the pages after your last page of text): epilogue, bibliography, references, appendices, and glossary.
- ☐ Photos (if you have any), scanned and saved to a disk.
- ☐ Photo captions.

Once you've compiled all the parts of your manuscript, send these materials with a note outlining what you've included. Your editor should not only edit and read over your manuscript, but also review all the accompanying parts. Last-minute additions that miss the editing process increase the risk of mistakes and inconsistencies.

 ## Need an ISBN?

If you plan to distribute your book to major booksellers or retailers, you'll need an ISBN (International Standard Book Number). An ISBN is the thirteen-digit number that identifies each book uniquely and connects it to a publisher; it's like your book's Social Security number. If you're establishing your own publishing company, your ISBN will be linked to your publishing company. If you hire a publishing company, they'll provide you with an ISBN. To purchase your ISBN, visit: www.myidentifiers.com, a subset of R.R. Bowker, the U.S. agency licensed to sell ISBNs. The current cost is $125.00 to purchase one ISBN and $250.00 to purchase ten. No, that's not a typo. The price for one is dramatically higher than buying in bulk. And you may as well buy in bulk, because each version or revised edition of your book, including different e-book formats, requires a new ISBN (for example, a new format or an expanded special edition). However, a subsequent printing where the book is identical to the original can keep the original ISBN.

How to Make a Good Book Great

Different editors have different editing processes. In my experience, editing electronically is the preference for most editors. Electronic editing is convenient for both the editor and author; it saves time and conserves money otherwise spent mailing manuscripts back and forth. In the electronic editing process, an editor typically uses Microsoft Word or another word-processing program and edits using the Track Changes feature, which highlights and underlines all changes made. Track Changes also allows editors to query and comment throughout the manuscript. As you go through your edited Microsoft Word document and review suggested changes from your editor, you have the option of accepting and rejecting each suggested change. If you accept, the change is permanently made. If you reject a change, your original copy remains untouched. You also have the option of clicking "Accept all changes in the document," but don't ever do that. Carefully review each change. It's your name on the cover. Editors are only human, and some of their recommendations may not suit your book.

While many editors edit manuscripts electronically, some editors—and authors—prefer editing on paper. A drawback to this approach is the task of entering each correction manually when you revise. I have to admit, although I love technology, I'm old-fashioned when it comes to editing. I happen to enjoy seeing edits in red ink on a hard copy! In writing this book, I used both methods.

As you review and make revisions, the best advice is to take your time. Don't rush, especially since this might be the last extensive round of changes you'll make to your manuscript. Don't cut corners, whatever your deadline may be. Rushing through editing and revisions is a valid pet peeve of editors.

If you're burned out and need to take a break from working on your manuscript, step away from revising until you have the energy and motivation to give it all you've got. Your editor may have suggestions for extensive rewriting, adding more content, or doing further fact checking that requires more research and thus more time. Don't make the mistake of getting lazy at this point. Do all that's needed to make your manuscript the best it can be and approach every suggestion with an open mind. A common misconception is that whatever is missed in editing and revising will be caught in proofreading, which isn't so. Proofreaders only catch typos, grammar mistakes, and misspellings—not content issues. A proofreader won't call attention to a factual inconsistency or anything related to content. **As you're revising your final draft, here's a checklist to refer to:**

☐ Make sure you're working from the final version of your manuscript when you begin revisions.

☐ Have your editor's style sheet, which is a guide created by the editor on general preferences, to make consistent changes throughout the manuscript.

☐ Have a hard copy of your manuscript with the editor's corrections (even if your manuscript was edited electronically).

☐ Make a list of (or mark with sticky notes in your hard copy) all the suggested changes that you don't agree with or need more clarification on and supply them to your editor for feedback.

☐ Keep a book on editing close by as a reference. Book editors and publishers use *The Chicago Manual of Style* and *Merriam-Webster's Manual for Writers & Editors*. Doing so will help guide you through understanding the editing marks and style corrections.

THE LAST WORD

- Don't expect an editor to do your writing; give your editor as complete a manuscript as possible that you've already reviewed thoroughly. Good editing enhances an already-strong manuscript.
- Remember that your editor should not compromise your voice, style, or creative vision in any way.
- Approach the editing process with the same care you did in the writing process. Editing is the most crucial step in pub-

lishing because it makes or breaks how well your writing comes across.

Indie Author Wisdom

"The greatest challenge for us was editing and fine tuning our visual ideas. A major mistake authors make is thinking they can finish the whole process in about half the time that they actually can...they find out they're wrong...over and over."

~Sara Jensen-Fritz, Thea Zitzow, and Paula Jones-Johnson, authors of *You and Your Military Hero* and *Every Kid's Guide to Living Your Best Life*

Design and Production: Preparing Your Book for the Market

Have you ever looked at a book and thought, *yikes! This book could look so much better?* Whether your readers encounter your book for sale on a physical shelf or a virtual shelf, design has the power to draw them in or turn them away. All books, including e-books, deserve and need good design.

I enjoy perusing bookstores for the sheer joy of scoping out books with eye-catching design. I gravitate to covers that are interesting with thoughtful graphics. I love an easy-to-read title that grabs me, and a color scheme that compliments the overall feel of the book. Books that aren't well designed usually have what I call "missing parts," such as readable fonts or more appealing colors to make the design come together. If your book's subject catches a reader's attention despite a poor design, the reader might still buy it. However, the key phrase is "catches a reader's attention." If a poorly designed book is displayed with other books on a similar subject, consumers will almost always choose a book that looks more attractive. I recently met a food stylist who artfully prepares the dishes that star in advertising and cookbook photo shoots. Something she said stuck with me. She explained that her career is vital to the food industry, because "people eat with their eyes first. If food doesn't look good, they won't eat it." This also applies to books. If a book doesn't look good, people won't spend money on it. Ken Thurber, author of *Big Wave Surfing: Extreme Technology, Management, Marketing & Investing*, shared,

> *From the start we did not perceive the book as simply a book, but rather a complete product requiring attention to every detail. In this vein every detail was implemented to ensure maximum consistency— down to the yellow thread in the binding matching the surf board on the cover. Overall, my book's design compliments the content by making it easy to read and navigate.*

Ken had the right idea. Though book design is the "fun part" of publishing and filled with excitement, it solidifies your book as a product. The details are important here. During the design phase, consider your brand as an author and the aesthetic style of your book, because these are the details that readers notice first.

This applies to e-books, too. Don't think you can skip this section because you only plan to sell a ninety-nine-cent e-book on Smashwords. You will need, at the least, an unforgettable cover. And while first-generation e-reader devices allowed for limited formatting, each new device that's released raises the bar for electronic publishing. Readers will be expecting not just pleasing design from their e-books, but hyperlinks, interactivity, and digital rewards yet to be discovered.

Get with a savvy designer if you want your e-book to be competitive.

Most authors need a little inspiration to get their creative juices flowing. Before any design meeting, I ask authors to select three or four of their favorite books and study their look and feel. Consider what elements lend credibility to books. What elements lessen the text's authority or make it look unprofessional? Don't think about *why* you like a particular book yet. Look for books that you're drawn to and find attractive, inside and out. Make a mental list of all the design details that you appreciate, such as color schemes, fonts, dimensions, use of graphics, and special details like callouts, pulled quotes, and dingbats (the graphic elements sometimes used to separate sections of text). Examine your list for distinct ideas to guide your book designer. A designer doesn't want to hear you say, "Just show me some concepts, I'll know it when I see it."

What Do Book Designers Do?

It's possible that you know at least one person who is a "designer." Perhaps you know an interior designer, a graphic designer, or a website designer. Book designers specifically design book covers and interiors. They're responsible for creating the concept for your cover and choosing the fonts, graphics, and overall design of the interior pages. Designers create your book's physical appearance, making sure every page projects a consistent impression, and prepare it for the printer or e-book distributor.

A common inaccuracy in self-publishing is that printers output whatever file format is supplied to them, such as a Microsoft Word doc. This is false. In order to produce books properly, book printers need special files specifically created by book designers using particular software programs. A true and experienced book designer is familiar with and uses software such as the Adobe Creative Suite on a regular basis. Adobe Creative Suite is a significant investment. It includes a number of complex design programs, and there is a learning curve.

For e-books, it gets more complicated. There's no current industry standard, which means multiple e-reading devices require multiple files. A good designer can output your manuscript into most or all of the files the market requires.

Hire an experienced professional rather than a beginner, and definitely don't design it yourself. Designers contribute invaluable ideas that enhance your project aesthetically. They're familiar with genres and trends in the market and know what questions to ask to create the right look and feel for your book. Their creativity is an asset, especially because readers often make buying decisions based as much on a book's design as on its content.

Here's how to know whether potential designers are skilled and competent enough to design your book:

- They supply samples of their work (preferably a printed book or portfolio of covers and interiors).
- Their samples are professional, attractive, and complement each book's content.
- They use current and up-to-date desktop-publishing software like Adobe Creative Suite.
- They're able to knowledgeably communicate with printers about paper stocks, cover finishes, cover laminations, bindings, and other specifications in book printing.

- They're willing and able to create a custom design for
  your book that doesn't look amateur.

What to Expect and How to Prepare for Working with Your Designer

The creative process is fruitful when the author and designer work together in a spirit of collaboration. As an author, you can prepare by reflecting on your vision for the book before your first design meeting. Authors often say that the design phase is one of their favorite parts of the publishing process—so savor it! If you're working with a self-publishing company, choose one that offers full and complete access to the book designer. You shouldn't be obliged to hand your book over to a person you're unable to collaborate with.

The point of self-publishing is to be involved in every facet of your book's development, from beginning to end, and that includes design. There should never be a person between you and your designer dictating preferences on your behalf. A good designer will enhance your publishing experience and might even join your network of key supporters.

Here's what you should provide to the designer:

- **A synopsis of your book:** Give your designer a written
  account of what your book is about, such as the copy that
  you intend to use for your book's back cover. Your designer
  won't read the entire book, so it's important that he or she
  has a synopsis that explains the book's selling points.

- **Biography:** Include a description of qualifications relevant to your book's topic, including your background, education, job experience, publications, and awards.
- **Endorsements:** Provide any testimonials that you've collected to be used on your cover.
- **A description of the intended audience:** Use lots of adjectives when describing your audience to the designer. Is the audience young and business-minded? Are your readers ready to retire? Is your book for parents of young children? Define your audience by interests, goals, expectations, and demographic variables of age, gender, income, and education. Get as specific as you can.
- **An explanation of your vision:** What kind of "feel" do you have in mind for the book? Let your designer know. Look online for book covers that you like and dislike. Print these out for the designer.
- **Final manuscript for text design phase:** The final manuscript must be complete before the book goes into design. Changes to the manuscript after page design increase time the designer has to spend laying out pages, which leads to increased costs.
- **Photographs:** If your book includes photos, organize them thoroughly. Use a sticky note on the back to mark each photo. For example, label the first photo in Chapter 1 this way: 1-1 Bob & Cindy. The numbers keep the photos in order and the short title describes the photo. If you provide digital or scanned photos: Use the same labeling system to name the files for each photo. Again, the numbers

keep the photos in order, and the short title describes the photo. The photos should be scanned as large as possible at 600 dpi and should be saved as a TIFF file.

- **Captions:** Provide your captions in a separate text file. They should be labeled to match the photo numbers. Have these edited and proofed along with your manuscript. If they're not edited, inconsistencies in spelling and punctuation may occur.
- **Graphics/charts/diagrams:** Provide graphics that have been scanned and saved digitally. If the designer is to create charts or diagrams, sketch and label what you want. Allow extra time for the designer to create these graphics.

What is "Good Design"?

The adage is true—readers will judge and buy books based on their covers. So, when it comes to the design of your book, don't cut corners. A number of elements contribute to a well-designed book. For starters, the design should be in harmony with the content and with the author's voice, not fighting against it. Good design enhances a book's content without overpowering it and makes the text more pleasurable to process. A well-designed book is readable, with simple text that is not overwrought with fancy, illegible fonts.

As you collaborate on your cover, pay attention to how easy or difficult it will be to see it from a distance. If your book is facing out on a shelf in a bookstore or library, you'll want the cover to be eye-catching. Opt for a cover with a clean design that isn't too busy with text or crowded with images, and display your title large and bold.

Design Process Outline:

1. Initial meeting with designer to discuss cover and text design ideas.
2. The designer works on designs. Sometimes the cover is first, other times text is first; other times the designer works on both simultaneously.
3. Author meets again with designer to review sample options. Usually there will be one text design, possibly with type variations, and one to three cover design options.
4. Author takes time to look at the designs and make comments or approve.
5. Author and designer meet, e-mail, and phone to discuss revisions (as necessary).
6. Author reviews and approves designs.
7. Designer receives final materials (edited Word doc, images, captions).
8. Production on text and cover begins.
9. Author, editor/proofreader, and publisher review round one, and return the proof to the designer.
10. Designer prepares final round.
11. Author and publisher review, and send manuscript to an indexer if needed (this round should have only minor corrections).
12. Designer places index, makes minor corrections.
13. Author gives final approval.
14. Designer sends files to printer.

Buyers typically look at books for an average of eight seconds. You want the title and cover to work together to draw in even the casual browsers. The mantra "less is more" especially applies here. Professional designers have a good eye for color, graphics, and fonts that work well together. Your job is to ensure that your book's design communicates its message effectively and that it isn't lost in translation. You can't predict how readers will respond to your book, but here's a glance at how marketers approach design, specifically color choices. I've added my spin on how to factor this into your book's design:

Black

Black signals authority, power, stability, and strength. Black is often chosen as a color to market luxury products and is also associated with intelligence (graduates in black robes and scholars in black-rimmed glasses). Books of a more serious nature such as business, self-help, and academic are known to heavily incorporate black. Black is also viewed as a somber color sometimes associated with darkness, and books in the suspense and thriller genres frequently feature black in their design. Because black is a serious color that induces strong emotions, it is easy to overwhelm readers with too much of it. I also find that books with black covers show differently on a computer screen than in person.

White

White is symbolic of hope, clarity, purity (wedding dresses, angels, and clouds), and cleanliness. White is also gender-neutral and frequently associated with creativity (white boards, blank slates). A heavy use of white comes across as clean and minimal, but runs the risk of appearing too basic and sterile. Lots of white space on a cover feels contemporary, inviting, and open.

Gray

Gray is conservative, no-nonsense, and timeless. Too much gray is dull and boring while the right amount adds solidarity and astuteness. Gray traditionally denotes old age, neutrality, death, depression, or loss of direction. Silver is an off-shoot of gray and often associated with a philanthropic and strong character.

Red

Red is the ultimate attention-grabbing color that is known to create a sense of urgency in buyers. It's a high-energy color associated with movement and excitement. Books with a hard-hitting message often have red prominent in their design. Red is also known to increase a person's heart rate. Many clever designers use a pop of red to make something important stand out. Red is considered the symbol of life, holidays, love, and revolution!

Pink

Pink, an offshoot of red, is perceived as calming, romantic, and feminine. Marketers traditionally use pink in products targeted to women and girls.

Blue

Blue is generally accepted as the favorite color of the masses. We're surrounded in blue—the sky, the ocean—and many bedrooms and bathrooms are decked in blue due to its ability to produce calming chemical agents. Blue is also known to prompt productivity and is connected to faithfulness, dependability, wisdom, and loyalty, hence the popularity of blue uniforms. Blue is heavily represented in books with patriotic, financial, and business themes. However, be aware that some shades (or too much blue) can feel cold.

Green

Green is known for being the easiest color for the eyes to process. It's the color of growth and nature—a popular choice for environmental messages. Green is shorthand for wealth and money, as well as a calming color associated with terms like rejuvenation and balance. Green is also connected to envy, good luck, generosity, fertility, peace, and harmony. Books with heavy greens are seen in genres like environment, health and wellness, finance, and spirituality.

Yellow

Yellow is the color of cheerfulness, laughter, optimism, and happiness. Yellow is known to release serotonin in the brain, has the power to increase metabolism, and produces creativity. When misused, yellow is overwhelming and provokes warning reactions—think "caution tape." However, yellow is most often perceived as a positive color and is seen frequently in products marketed to children.

Orange

Orange is associated with fun, energy, and warmth. It is also associated with ambition and innovation. Marketers frequently use orange to send the "buy" message as it is known to attract impulse buyers. Orange, like red, has the ability to overpower in large doses, but in the right shade and used strategically it has high impact abilities. A person in marketing and product development also noted that orange is the most "polarizing" color, in that it is equally loved and hated.

Purple

Purple is the color of royalty, wealth, prosperity, and elegance. Purple is a stimulating color, known to evoke calm and also lend an air of mystery and respect. Purple is known to be a favorite of young girls, but is also used heavily in beauty- and women-related books. Both purple and its pastel, lavender, are also associated with the GLBT community.

Brown

Brown is the color of reliability, stability, and friendship. Books of an earthy or outdoorsy nature often use heavy brown undertones. Some shades of brown, such as beige or taupe, do run the risk of erring on the dull side. However, because of its neutral nature brown is a popular color choice across all genres.

What Designers Want You to Know

Award-winning book designer Ryan Scheife advises that there is no right or wrong way to design a book cover. As with all art, the cover will draw varied subjective opinions, depending on who is viewing it. However, when creating your book's cover, remember that your designer has a specific intent and puts the various elements together for a reason. Scheife's advice: Use caution when tweaking your cover design. Make sure you're happy with the proposal, but trust that your designer is a professional who knows the principles of good design.

Follow this checklist for offering creative input when working with a designer (use for your e-book, as well):

- ☐ **Follow standard design conventions**: It's good to be different, but your book shouldn't stand out for the wrong reasons. If there's a standard size and format within your book's genre, don't veer too far away from that. Think of your customer and their preferences.
- ☐ **Choose readable fonts**: With countless fonts to choose from, there will certainly be a number of directions your book's design could take. Regardless of style preferences, make sure your fonts are readable. Don't alternate between more than three fonts within your book. For your book's interior, most readers prefer serif fonts like Times New Roman or Garamond. For e-books, Verdana and Georgia are considered the most readable on computer screens. Avoid gaudy or unprofessional fonts, such as Lucida Handwriting or Comic Sans. One book reviewer

shared that she won't touch a book with even a title in either of those fonts.

☐ **Check the trends**: Book design evolves constantly. What was trendy five years ago is not the case today. Pay attention to the design trends within your book's genre and digest them. Possible trends might include lots of white space and minimal text, illustrated graphics, or more serious fonts versus casual fonts.

Scheife also shared that new authors should give thought to the images they track down for use in their book. "Typically, images that are pulled from the web are not a good idea," he cautions. "There are always usage rights and resolution issues to consider with graphics you plan to include in your book." In using photos, Scheife advises using originals that add a personal touch to your book. "I'm always excited when an author comes armed with images for me to pull from for the design. However, if you'll be relying on stock images—either for your cover or for elements within the interior—it's probably best to leave the researching and purchasing of images to your designer." The reasonable cost, wide variety, and high-quality standards of stock images can add a lot to your book's design.

Advice for Your Back-Cover or Front-Flap Copy

The best advice for writing effective back-cover copy is to always keep in mind how your book will help or entertain your audience. Imagine your reader picking up your book and wondering, "What's this book about and why should I buy it?" Make your copy simple, and clear. Don't oversell. Your back-cover copy should communicate what it will deliver and be free of jargon. Avoid catch phrases that are empty value judgments, like *ground-breaking* and *cutting-edge*.[5] And do your readers a favor—don't write an overly long summary. The average book shopper only looks at the back cover for a few seconds. The back-cover copy must state the problem and explain how your book will empower the reader with solutions. Highlight the most interesting qualities of your book that you know your audience will love. Don't make them work too hard to figure out what your book is about and why they should want it.

For fiction, the back-cover copy has to grab the reader's attention right away with a captivating plot description that doesn't give too much of the story away. Be provocative when describing your book and use words that engage the senses. Show your reader what the book is about by addressing the action, drama, intrigue, and controversy in the story. Don't simply list the facts about it. Here's my list of tips for creating effective back-cover copy for fiction writers:

- Introduce the main character(s) and the major conflict in the story.
- Describe the obstacles and strengths of the main character(s).
- Include a vague hint of the climax.
- Create a sense of mystique; build anticipation.
- Use descriptive language that sets the mood and tone of the book.
- Avoid the following words: *best, greatest, most excellent,* or other superlatives that oversell without describing the story.

Below is an example of back-cover copy for a fiction title that effectively tells buyers enough without saying too much:

An ardent young woman, her cowardly lover, and her aging, vengeful husband—these are the central characters in this stark drama of the conflict between passion and convention in the harsh, Puritan world of seventeenth-century Boston.

The description is for *The Scarlet Letter,* the classic novel by Nathaniel Hawthorne, and it follows all the rules with being short at only thirty-six words, introduces the intrigue of the main characters (a young woman, her lover, and her husband) and the propelling conflict (passion vs. convention).

Proofreading Your Book

After your book is designed, it is should be proofread—without question. Proofreading is an absolute must, even for short books with little text. By the end of the publishing process your book will have been examined so many times that you may think proofreading is unnecessary. However, as the author, your eyes have grown used to the content. You'll probably miss mistakes, or introduce new ones, after incorporating your editor's suggestions.

A proofreader, like an editor and book designer, is a trained professional with a talent for finding mistakes, errors, incorrect punctuation, and misspellings. And yes, even with a word processor's spelling and grammar check, typos find their way into books all the time. For example, the grammar checker in Microsoft Word sees nothing wrong with this title: *Why Less Students Are Getting Threw College in For Years.* A proofreader, depending on the size of your book, should turn around corrections in five to ten business days. Some proofreaders charge by the hour, while others charge by the word. Expect your proofreader to do the following:

- Read the entire manuscript for errors in spelling, grammar, and punctuation.
- Double check the page numbers listed in your table of contents against the actual pages.
- Verify that all the accompanying pieces to the text, such as photos, graphs, and tables, are present and properly identified.

Once the proofreader is done with your book, carefully review corrections and make sure there aren't suggestions with which you disagree. You don't want to be surprised by a change you had no idea was implemented. Once you've approved your proofreader's corrections, your designer makes those changes—and off you go to the printer!

Finalizing Your Book for the Printer

While working with your book designer, you're essentially preparing your book for the press. During this stage, ensure that you've provided everything that he or she needs and that all final changes have been made. Doublecheck the proofreader's corrections against the final version of your book to make sure all corrections were implemented.

Proofreader's Marks

Symbol	Meaning	Example
ℬ or ᵟ or ᵍ	delete	take ℓ out
○	close up	print as o ne word
ℬ	delete and close up	clo se up
∧ or > or ∧	caret	insert here (something
#	insert a space	put one here
eq#	space evenly	space evenly ∧ where indicated
stet	let stand	let marked text stand as set
tr	transpose	change order the
/	used to separate two or more marks and often as a concluding stroke at the end of an insertion	
[	set farther to the left	⌐ too far to the right
]	set farther to the right	too⌐ far to the left
⌒	set as ligature (such as)	encyclopaedia
=	align horizontally	alignment
‖	align vertically	‖ align with surrounding text
×	broken character	imperfect
□	indent or insert em quad space	
¶	begin a new paragraph	
⊛	spell out	set 5 lbs. as five pounds
cap	set in CAPITALS	set nato as NATO
sm cap or s.c.	set in SMALL CAPITALS	set signal as SIGNAL
lc	set in lowercase	set South as south

Proofreader's Marks (continued)

ital	set in *italic*	set oeuvre as *oeuvre*
rom	set in roman	set *mensch* as mensch
bf	set in **boldface**	set important as **important**
= or -/ or ⌢ or /H/	hyphen	multi-colored
⌐/N or *en* or /N/	en dash	1965–72
⌐/M or *em* or /M/	em (or long) dash	Now—at last!—we know.
∨	superscript or superior	as in πr^2
∧	subscript or inferior	as in H_2O
∧∨ or ∨∧	centered	for a centered dot in $p \cdot q$
⋏	comma	
⋎	apostrophe	
⊙	period	
; or ;/	semicolon	
: or ⊙	colon	
❨❩ or ⋎⋎	quotation marks	
(/)	parentheses	
[/]	brackets	
OK/?	query to author: has this been set as intended?	
⊥ or ⊥¹	push down a work-up	an unintended mark
⑤¹	turn over an inverted letter	inverted
*wf*¹	wrong font	wrong siZe or stylℓ

Back-Cover Copy Outline for Nonfiction Authors:

Headline: What will a reader get from your book? What is the question your reader needs answered?

Testimonials (Optional): Two or three statements from industry insiders that will add authority to your book.

Summary: Begin with a declarative statement about the problem or subject that your book addresses. Follow with a statement about how *your book* specifically solves, confronts, or shows the reader how to overcome this problem. Follow this with a statement that declares your book's unique position on the topic. Sell your book plainly and directly with a statement about how readers will be able to use your book's content.

Author Biography: Show your unique qualifications for writing the book. Include hands-on experience, previously published books on the topic, awards in your industry, and current work projects related to the topic. Only include details that are relevant to the book's content. However, it's not a bad idea to include one or two lighthearted facts (e.g., your dog's name, hometown, hobby).

Before your designer submits the final files, do the following:

- Confirm that all the components of your book, such as the front cover, ISBN, barcode, copyright page, publication date, back-cover copy, book price, testimonials, front matter, back matter, and author biography, have been proofread and are included in the design.
- Look through the entire final manuscript to ensure all of the proofreader's corrections have been added.
- Discuss and finalize your book specifications (trim size, cover treatments, paper color, etc.).
- Discuss and finalize unique or unusual aspects of the print job (embossing, French flaps, foil treatments, etc.).

Your designer will provide the files to the printer. Most designers send printer-ready PDFs, fonts, links, and the native files (the files saved in its original format, such as InDesign or Illustrator files). The designer will be involved through the printing process and will probably communicate with the printer on your behalf. If adjustments are needed at the printing stage, such as increasing the resolution of a photo or making other minor tweaks to the files, your designer should be able to resolve them for you.

To Galley or Not to Galley?

Many authors don't consider their book complete until they've snagged a glowing blurb from a celebrity or well-known person affiliated with their book's subject. Readers do pay attention to books that are endorsed by people they respect. Publicist Rachel Anderson agreed, saying:

> *Book endorsements are great to have. They raise the level of credibility for an author. If, for example, you have a book about organ donation and it is endorsed by the American Kidney Association, its value to potential readers instantly goes up. As a result, it will be easier for the author to get the book carried on that organization's website, and they'll have a better chance of getting a booth at an event sponsored by the organization.*

So how do you get the right people to offer a blurb for your book? One way is to send out galleys. A *galley proof* or *galley*, also referred to as an a*dvanced reader copy* or *ARC*, is a bound proof of your manuscript. It looks like a book with a cover and book binding, except there's usually a notice on the front cover that reads "Uncorrected Bound Galleys. Not For Sale." Most galleys are printed while your book is with the proofreader, so they're expected to have a few errors. While most indie authors print galleys professionally, con-

> **Most galleys are printed while your book is with the proofreader, so they're expected to have a few errors.**

sider having a local copier bind your manuscript inexpensively with a spiral. Either way, having something to send to a potential endorser is the best way to get good blurbs.

Another efficient possibility is a digital galley (for strict e-book publishing, it's the only possibility!). Many authors use a combination of print and digital. When putting out feelers, ask your potential endorsers if they'd rather read your galley on paper, or download it onto their Kindle, Nook, iPad, or other device. Your designer can help you create a file in the correct format for the device, or you can try a service like netgalley.com.

Netgalley.com is worth exploring for a lot of reasons, including the chance to see up-and-coming projects by other authors. Like anything else, you get out of it what you put into it. Uploading your manuscript to Netgalley.com doesn't make it likely that a bored *New York Times* book reviewer will stumble across your work and give it a fabulous review. You've got to be strategic. Go after the people you've got a chance of getting to.

If you do decide to print galleys to collect blurbs for your book in advance, you'll need to factor it into your schedule and allot the appropriate amount of time. Printing a galley takes two weeks or less; however, e-mailing, mailing, and following up with your contacts about potential endorsements can be time consuming. Most major book review publications such as *Kirkus* or *Publishers Weekly* will require a galley ninety days before your book is published. Give this process at least two months. Galleys work best when you know who to contact and have the means to reach those people. If you don't know who to approach for an endorsement, galleys are useless.

Here's a checklist if you decide to print galleys:

☐ Create a wish list of endorsers as soon as possible.
☐ Include people you see as long shots (celebrities and industry experts).

☐ Compile the contact information for each endorser.

☐ Use social media sites such as Twitter, Facebook, and LinkedIn to find and contact endorsers.

☐ Organize a schedule of deadlines to send your book to review publications.

☐ Time your galley printing with your book going to the proofreader.

☐ Prepare "ready-made" testimonials in case an endorser is too busy to generate one for you. An example is, "Bottom line: I highly recommend *Title* for _____ who want the perfect resource for _____" and "If you want to be _____, you need the expertise of _____. *Title* is filled with valuable tools and priceless knowledge."

☐ Only print the number of galleys that you truly need (Most authors print ten to twenty-five).

☐ Give endorsers a firm deadline and hold them to it. If they don't meet it, move on.

THE LAST WORD

- The design phase of publishing should only happen once the manuscript is final—no buts!
- Your book's design should reflect your vision—do all you can to show and explain it to your designer of choice.
- When building your book, look closely to determine if there is flexibility in the schedule to print galleys for advanced review.

- Your manuscript must be proofread by a professional.
- PDFs also work as galleys and save print costs.

Indie Author Wisdom

"I've found the greatest benefit of being an author is knowing that we're impacting and touching the lives of young people and honoring their sacrifice. Whether I've spoken to an audience of one thousand people or two people, I've helped someone."

~DeAnne Sherman, co-author of *Finding My Way*, *You Are Not Alone*, and *My Story*

Printing Your Book

When looking at printers, you'll need to make some important decisions about the format (paperback or hardcover), trim size, paper, and cover material. Thousands of printers are at your disposal. Keep in mind that printers offer varying degrees of quality, speed, and knowledge.

Work exclusively with a book printer, often referred to as a book manufacturer. A book printer will cost less than a printer whose specialty is print advertisements, catalogs, or other promotional materials. Do your research and request samples of the printer's work ahead of time. Book printers are happy to supply samples of printed books and can help you make decisions about paper stock, cover coating, and bindings. If you can, work with a printer within driving distance of where you live, and you'll save money on shipping. If your printer is close enough, arrange for a press check to visit during the proofing stage to get a more hands-on proofing experience. If you're working with a publisher, you'll have access to experienced printers and will be shown samples prior to making a selection.

Most printers will work with novices who are not familiar with book printing, but they naturally prefer to work with publishers or designers with the knowledge, expertise, and ability to troubleshoot issues that might occur during the printing process. That being said, more printers than ever enthusiastically help authors self-publish, and many even offer services such as editing, design, and proofreading. Be careful to note the quality of such printers, and if you'd like to take them up on their editing and design services, always ask for samples of their work first.

Book Specifications

You'll often hear the term "specs" when you send your book to press. Specs, short for "specifications," are the important details of your book, such as size, binding, and paper color. You might already have a general idea of your book's physical appearance, or you may make these decisions with a designer. Your decisions might also come down to cost. Pay attention to the standards for your genre and your audience's expectations. For instance, children's picture books are usually hardcovers printed in color. Memoirs and novels are printed in black and white and work well as paperbacks.

Pay attention to the standards for your genre and your audience's expectations.

Trim Size

Trim size is the width and height of a book. Printers have precut paper available in bulk for standard trim sizes. When choosing a trim size that isn't standard, the printer has to special order the paper, which will increase costs. Standard sizes are 5.5" × 8.5", 6" × 9", and 8.5" × 11". Novels, memoirs, and biographies are 5.5" × 8.5" and 6" × 9"; standard children's picture books are 8.5" × 11" and 11" × 8.5".

Bindings

The standard binding for paperback books is referred to as a "perfect binding," where a book's pages are glued into the spine. When producing a hardcover book, you can choose between a few different bindings of varying costs. The standard binding for hardcover books was "smythe sewn" bindings (also referred to as "section sewn"), with pages sewn and glued into the spine. This binding was once considered the sturdiest option for a hardcover book. Smythe sewn is now rarely used unless requested. For a hardcover, your best option is "adhesive case" binding or "burst binding," which combines the cost savings of a perfect bind with the protection of a hardcover case; in this format, the pages are glued into the spine like a perfect bind with a hardcover case attached.

Paper Stock

Choosing the interior paper stock for your book boils down to the type of book you have. For novels, memoirs, biographies, and most nonfiction, the paper stock is what's called sixty-pound offset paper. Sixty-pound offset paper is the standard or "house" stock at most printers and will usually be the most cost-effective option. For coffee-table books, children's picture books, and other full-color books, coated paper (usually at least an eighty-pound gloss paper stock) is the accepted norm, because a heavier weight holds the ink and complements the art.

You have other paper options, and the best way to learn of them is to request samples from your printer. You can choose paper stocks in different colors, but despite the range, white and natural are the two most common options. Natural is the tan or cream-colored paper you see most in fiction books and many memoirs, biographies, and inspirational books. Natural paper is easier on the eyes than stark white, so consider natural for books with pure text. However, if your book has illustrations or black and white photographs, white paper is best.

Covers

If your book is a paperback, the standard cover stock is 10 pt. C1S (ten point coated on one side). If you want a thicker stock, increase the weight of the paper to 12 pt. or even higher, but again, ask to see samples of the stock in advance. Paperback covers have either a gloss lamination or matte lamination. While gloss is more common, matte offers a pleasant tactile experience and has recently become extremely popular. However, matte is slightly more expensive than gloss.

Hardcovers come with more choices to consider. Hardcovers typically have dust jackets, which means decisions must be made about paper stock and coatings for the jacket, as well as about the case itself. For hardcover books, most printers have a standard or "house" stock that's the most cost-effective option, usually in varying colors. Aside from the standard case stock, linens and papers are also options. Most hardcover cases display the title and author name in foiled lettering on the front and spine.

Dust jackets, a removable sheet with flaps used to cover hardcovers, are typically made with eighty-pound paper and, like paperbacks, can be coated with a gloss or matte lamination. Some hardcovers have a wrapped hardcover rather than a cloth case and dust jacket. In this style, the cover consists of a heavily coated paper stock "wrapped" onto the cover case rendering the dust jacket optional since the wrapped cover displays the design. Children's books and textbooks are good candidates for this option. If you decide to have a dust jacket as well, it usually replicates the design of the wrapped cover.

The Deal with Print-On-Demand

The term *print-on-demand* (POD) describes a few different processes. POD is often used interchangeably with the term *short-run printing*, or printing in small numbers. POD also describes the method of printing books individually as consumers place orders. Both methods allow an indie author, or even traditional publisher, to control printing and warehousing costs. A printing company that specializes in small print runs and POD services offers faster turnaround than an offset printer. Offset printers specialize in printing high volumes at a lower cost per book, usually starting at one thousand books. POD printers print as few books as you need, even if it's just one copy. POD books are usually printed using digital technology, which continues to get better, meaning that your book's quality shouldn't suffer. But, as always, ask for samples!

Publishers often use POD to create bound galleys, keep out-of-print books in stock, and print books that have a small niche audience.[6] Indie authors use POD to keep costs low, especially if their book caters to a small niche audience. If you only need two hundred books initially, why print two thousand? However, because POD machines operate more like a copy machine than the sophisticated printers of larger presses, POD is not recommended for hardcover children's picture books, coffee-table books, or books that rely heavily on images to communicate content.

The unit price per book decreases significantly as the quantity increases. For a one-hundred-fifty-page, 6" × 9" paperback, you might pay fifteen dollars per book at a quantity of fifty books. That same book printed at a quantity of 1,000 might cost you five dollars per book. The most common print quantities for POD printing are between twenty and five hundred. After a print run of five hundred, it becomes more cost effective to switch to an offset printer.

As an indie author, you set the timeline and the rules, so POD is an especially neat option for "sales testing." If you're not sure that you'd be able to sell a thousand or more books, why not experiment with a smaller inventory? Get a feel for the market and test how well you'll be able to create demand. As your quantity dwindles, print more copies on an as-needed basis, all the while lowering your sales risks. POD has long been a successful method for authors who want to see their work in print at a low cost, and some authors even use their POD books to score book deals with larger publishers.

As we now live in the world of Amazon, which is the major seller of hard copy books, it is worth noting that you now have the option of publishing your paper book with a print-on-demand (POD) company that will take care of worldwide distribution without ever forcing you to warehouse books. Lightning Source, a subsidiary of Ingram, is one such company. While it is possible to make these books returnable in order to increase your chances of selling them in brick and mortar bookstores, I don't advise it—you would be responsible for the printing cost of any copies returned, and when you have not paid for printing up front, being struck with 5,000 returns at $5 per copy would be no fun indeed! Even so, POD is a great option for authors seeking worldwide distribution without having to pay printing costs up front.

THE LAST WORD

- It's always a good idea to select the book specifications that not only complement your budget but also best serve your audience—do your research on these two factors before talking to printers.
- Take a trip to a local printing press and experience an up-close view of how a book comes together.
- Request samples from your printer of choice to make sure the quality is up to speed.
- If you have a small, niche audience or if you're not completely confident in your marketing strategy, consider using print-on-demand as a way to test the market.

Indie Author Wisdom

"My advice to someone self-publishing: pray a lot first! I really did pray about it. Pray hard and work like hell!"

~Suzanne Ruff, author of *The Reluctant Donor*

Distributing Your Printed Book to the Marketplace

Distribution is possibly the least exciting yet most important challenge that indie authors face for electronic and printed books. E-books have the advantage here, with new distribution avenues opening up each day (that's covered in a later chapter). For print books, the game hasn't changed much since the Great Depression, except for the fact that there are fewer and fewer bookstores. That's the bad news. The good news is that traditional authors are in the same boat, but you as an indie author won't live in fear of your publisher banishing your book to the backlist the minute sales weaken. Like the tortoise and the hare, you can roll it out slowly and strategically while the traditional author has to expend and sustain a big burst of energy to stay in the race.

In my work, I've discovered that indie authors effortlessly sell the first hundred books by hand to their various networks. At a book launch party, I once witnessed an author sell two hundred books to family and friends alone. Savvy indie authors sell books directly to readers as often as possible. However, dependable distribution outside of direct sales is crucial to a book's success. One bookstore buyer explained:

> *Indie books, unlike traditional books, don't catch in the market until the sixth or seventh month of being published. Sales increase over time, which is why I recommend indie authors have a means to accommodate bookstore buyers, online book retailers, and wholesalers. If your book grows a following from grassroots marketing, there has to be a way for readers to find and buy the book.*

Her comments are not only correct, but telling. Printed book distribution is the main dividing line between self-publishing and traditional publishing. We've talked about the benefits of self-publishing, such as complete creative control and potentially higher profits. When it comes to print, bookstore distribution is the primary wall that self-publishers must climb. Knowing this upfront helps you not only prepare, but also have a strategy to guarantee your book doesn't fall into the "unreachable" category. For the record, even small traditional presses face challenges entering major distribution channels. Though you could depend solely on readers who buy books online, your book in a brick-and-mortar store is an eye-catching advertisement.

You may have heard that bookstores are snobby about self-published books and are adamantly against carrying them. While there is occasional truth to this, in reality bookstores don't want to risk taking a loss on your book, especially when they can't rely on it being promoted by established publishers. Bookstores almost always require that a publisher take back unsold books. Traditionally, POD and self-published copies are considered "non-returnable." Most bookstores won't take the chance on a self-published book that can't be purchased through their wholesaler of choice (at a discount) and returned if it doesn't sell. Fortunately, demand opens doors at booksellers.

Avert roadblocks by simply knowing how the distribution channels work. Hiring a mentoring press that has established relationships with reputable book wholesalers is one way to navigate the system. Another option is visiting every bookstore within driving distance and selling your books to them on a consignment basis, meaning you're paid only when a book is sold within a predetermined period, the average being ninety days. Take into account that bookstores are historically supportive of local writers, especially writers who've done their research and understand how bookstore retail works. If you're planning to have your book available outside of your city or state, here are some tips:

- Consider smaller print runs, with your unit cost low enough to make a profit *and* not take a hit if your books get returned.
- Have your marketing plan ready before pitching to bookstores. The more confidence a bookstore has in your marketing efforts, the better. A well-rounded marketing campaign should include direct-to-reader marketing, radio appearances, articles, and events.
- Show your cover designs to bookstores before going to print. Bookstores especially judge a book by its cover.

If you intend to hire a self-publishing company and you want national distribution for your book, make sure the company has the means to help warehouse your book copies, fulfill orders via the web and phone, and has access to bookstore wholesalers such as Ingram and Baker & Taylor. These should be built-in services that are either included in your chosen package or available as add-ons.

Bookstore sales increase access to your book but add two degrees of separation between you and your readers. A disadvantage of bookstores is that they can demand a maximum discount of 55 percent off your book's selling price. Selling books directly to readers at book fairs, seminars, workshops, book launches, discussions, signings, and through your personal website means you receive the entire cover price. Weigh your sales goals, book's mission, and marketing plans to determine which distribution track makes the most sense for you. As an indie author, you're unlimited in the ways you can reach your audience. Besides bookstores, gift shops, and other retailers relevant to your book, the most logical distribution channels are:

- Selling directly to your readers
- Amazon.com
- Appearances, classes, presentations, and speaking engagements

Navigating the World of Returns

When bookstores order books, they can return unsold books for credit against future orders for up to a year. Returned books are shipped out again when another bookstore orders them. The downer about returns for indie authors is that it is downright frustrating to find that, after believing you've sold a certain number of books, a box or two might come back. You'll also typically have to wait thirty or even sixty days from the time of an order before receiving funds from book-stores to ensure they've sold your stock.

If they haven't sent you funds, then they haven't sold their cop-ies—that's where the returns come in. This practice keeps bookstores from taking losses on books and is a huge reason for you to pro-mote your book to the fullest. If you don't direct traffic to book-stores and create demand, they'll send inventory back to where it came from. The good news is that smaller and independent publishers (this includes you) have fewer returns compared to larger publishers[7], because independently published books are less likely to oversaturate the bookstore market. Returns usually happen when too many copies are pushed through the bookstore market and the demand isn't there. If you focus most of your efforts on nontrade sales (such as direct sales, special sales to businesses and organizations, and sales at speak-ing engagements), you'll be spared the stress of returns. Returns are an expensive nuisance and a necessary evil, so while you can't completely eliminate them, here are some tips on how they can be avoided:

- **Print a reasonable number of books:** The authors I work with often begin with one thousand copies and reprint after selling their initial inventory. Ordering a small number allows you to test the market without get-ting in over your head.
- **Set the right price for your book:** Overpricing is the number-one complaint from bookstores about self-pub-

lished books. If your book is priced too high, readers will simply not buy it, especially if there is a comparable book available for less.

- **Promote, promote, promote:** If bookstores know that you're out there marketing and sending customers to their stores, they'll be more supportive and are less likely to send your books back. Also, if you have a book signing at a store, let your network know you'll be there. Bookstores love authors who bring in buyers.

- **Monitor your inventory and sales before reprinting:** Be careful about reprinting unless you have marketing strategies in place, secured future orders, and have been paid for the inventory carried in stores.

- **Partner with independent bookstores:** Some indie bookstores will take books on consignment directly from authors. They'll usually want a sixty-forty split: 60 percent to you, 40 percent to them, which is standard in the book trade. Independent bookstores typically take between two and five copies until they see demand, but they are traditionally more supportive of indie authors, especially those who are local.

In addition to these tips, I agree with the method that Steve Carlson of Upper Access, Inc., Book Publishers uses in his approach to returns:

I haven't given up on trade sales. When a new title comes out, I encourage my distributor to place it in as many stores as possible. Of course, that is a risky proposition. Thousands of books are placed in stores, and any of them that don't sell within a matter of months will be returned.

If my early publicity is successful, there won't be many books coming back. But if early publicity fails—and once in a while it does—a big percentage come back. I could reduce that risk by telling my distributor to place the book in fewer stores. But I'm willing to take the risk because having more books in stores helps overall sales, and the returns are a cost of doing business. Once a title has been out for a while, bookstores reorder only as many as they figure they can sell.

How much each partner makes from a typical indie book sale:

	Price	Author	Wholesaler	Bookstore
Direct	$20	$20 (100 percent)	$0	$0
Book Retailers	$20	$9 (45 percent)	$3 (15 percent)	$8 (40 percent)
Website/PayPal	$20	$19.40 (Minus Service Fee)	$0	$0

Pricing Your Book Correctly

The price of your book is both a business and marketing decision and usually set in the design phase. At that point, you'll know the costs of producing your book after making final decisions about size, binding, and print run. Select a price that recoups your investment without overpricing the book. If your book is priced too high, bookstores will be reluctant to purchase it, and so will your readers. However, pricing your book too low impacts your bottom line. Here are some questions that you'll need to ask yourself:

- What are your competitors charging?
- What are your fixed and variable costs?
- What is your break-even point?

The two models that indie authors should consider when evaluating the price of their books are market-based pricing and perceived-value pricing. With market-based pricing, you'll compare other books in the same genre to your book and let that act as a deciding factor for your book's list price. This method is more reactive and lets the decision of your book price be determined, ultimately, by someone else. But it also allows you to set a price lower than the competition's, giving your book the advantage. Find a balance between securing profit and staying competitive.

Perceived-value pricing is considered the highest profit strategy; however, the benefits are usually most visible in the short-term. With this method, you price your book at what you believe your readers are willing to pay. This strategy works best for business authors or books that complement a known or established brand. The perceived-value strategy works particularly well for consultants or self-employed individuals with a growing consumer base. In this case, a book with a high price tag increases the value in a consumer or client's mind, working to the author's advantage. Authors of fiction, memoirs, children's fiction, and poetry should avoid this method of pricing—these genres sell to the most cost-conscious buyers.

Accepting Credit Cards

We're in the age of plastic, and accepting credit cards for a book sale is mandatory. You'll need to have your book on a website—either your own or an online retailer's—that will accept credit cards as a form of payment. Accepting credit cards increases cash flow, and payment is placed quickly and conveniently in your account, usually within forty-eight hours. In addition to offering books online, many authors set up merchant accounts to accept credit card payments at conferences, trade shows, and speaking engagements. Although processing fees range up to 3 percent, at least you won't miss out on customers who don't have cash; and fewer and fewer people carry cash these days.

> In addition to offering books online, many authors set up merchant accounts to accept credit card payments on the spot at conferences, trade shows, and speaking engagements.

The most popular merchant account for authors is PayPal (www.paypal.com), which has no up-front or monthly fees, has a swipe fee of 2.9 percent, and is easily integrated into websites. PayPal offers various levels of service, including a shopping cart feature that enables readers to purchase books easily and securely. A favorite feature of mine is the "virtual terminal" which operates similarly to a cash register. When you're at an event, PayPal's virtual terminal allows you to enter your customer's credit card information. All you need is a laptop and WiFi. Another tool for accepting credit card payments is Square (www.squareup.com). Square works with Android-based devices, iPhones, or iPads. Once you sign up for their free service, you'll receive a device by mail that allows you to swipe credit cards. It's a simple process that only requires signing up, downloading the Square application onto your phone or tablet, and plugging the Square reader into your device's headphone jack. The swipe fees are currently 2.75 percent compared to PayPal's 2.9 percent.

The number of books you sell shouldn't be limited to the amount of cash customers have on hand. Increasing your ability to take credit card orders on the fly by signing up for a merchant account is an important way to reap the benefits of direct sales.

Before selecting a merchant account provider other than Square and PayPal, double check the following:

- Strict security processes offered, such as encrypted transactions
- Protection against fraud and stolen or expired cards
- Customer service that can be contacted twenty-four-seven in case of an emergency
- Systems in place for returns and transaction disputes
- Quick turnaround on sales reaching accounts
- The ability to monitor accounts online

THE LAST WORD

- Distribution is the key to sales—without it, readers can't access your book.
- Be patient once your book is working through the wholesalers and bookstore channels; it takes months to know how many books were sold and not returned.

- Use several different methods to distribute your book, including selling directly to readers. It's good to interact with readers for marketing purposes, and direct sales also increase your profit margin.
- Offer your buyers the option to pay with a credit card, especially when you're face-to-face with them.

Indie Author Wisdom

"Do your homework and due diligence. Don't be afraid to ask questions. Also realize that self-publishing is going to be an expensive project without any guarantees. Keep your enthusiasm through the process and be gutsy."

~Patrick "Packy" Mader, author of the
Opa and Oma series and *Big Brother Has Wheels*

E-Books—Leading the Revolution

For the record, I was one of the wary who dreaded any movement away from traditional books. From the mid-1990s to early 2000s, when e-books were declared the next epic technology and a major threat to printed books, I scoffed and not-so-secretly wished they'd disappear. When forecasters predicted that electronic books would affect the book market the way MP3s did the music industry, I vowed to stay true to "tree" books, especially given the unforeseen challenges with usability and the high cost of e-readers. Fast forward to today, and I love my e-reader. I received it as a birthday gift, and while I still hold printed books near and dear, I can't deny that e-books changed my reading experience—for the better. And there's no denying the tremendous benefit of e-books to indie authors.

Current e-reading devices and tablets are more like miniature computers or all-purpose tools for viewing content, and the convenience factor appeals to the masses. The varieties of e-readers offered provide readers of all demographics plenty of options to suit their preferences.

As a result, e-books are getting more and more of the limelight in the publishing world. E-book sales have doubled in the last year, especially in the adult fiction category.[8] Big publishers have found that e-books benefit their processes, reduce waste, and decrease book warehousing requirements.[9] Indie authors are in an even better position than larger houses to exploit the digital trends in publishing. If you haven't considered creating an e-book version of your book, now is the time to take a serious look at doing so. Though you might initially feel overwhelmed trying to understand the lingo, processes, formats, and options—and you're not alone—the technology and services for authors continue to grow and become easier by the day. My caution, which won't surprise you, is to keep quality as a priority. There seems to be a large quantity of e-books in the marketplace with errors, poor cover designs (or no cover at all!) and an absence of editing.

What Is an E-Book?

Similar to the terms *self-publishing* and *print-on-demand*, the term *e-book* has varying definitions. Sometimes the term simply refers to a PDF. Other times an e-book includes any digital content developed by book publishers that can be viewed online. According to Outsell, Inc., an e-book is "a downloadable unit of book content that is readable on a variety of devices [e.g., e-readers, computers, or smartphones]."

To create an e-book, publishers start with the final edited text and a cover design (although cover design is not required, it is preferred). The text can be a PDF, an Adobe InDesign file, or any word processing document. The text is then converted into an ePub file and/or a Mobi/KF8 file. These programs present stripped-down versions of the text, sans most design elements. After the ePub file is approved for publication by the publisher or author, it is then uploaded to e-book vendors' sites. It can be viewed in Adobe Digital Editions, which is a free software download at Adobe's website (www.adobe.com/products/digital editions). While some e-book distributors like Smashwords require that their ePub and Mobi/KF8 files be generated from specially formatted Microsoft Word documents, authors can also pay for custom designed e-books that they can upload directly to all of the major vendors' self-publishing portals. All of the world's major e-book vendors have self-publishing portals that allow authors to work with them directly. Amazon uses a program called Kindle Direct Publishing, Barnes & Noble uses PubIt!; Kobo uses Writing Life, and Apple uses Apple Publishing and iTunes Producer. The only caveat to working directly with Apple is that you must be a Mac user. If you don't have a Mac, it will be necessary to use a third-party aggregator such as Smashwords, Lulu, or Ingram. One benefit of using distributors like these is that they do make your e-book available in some of the less prominent channels. Even so, they all take a portion of your profits. The majority of readers purchase e-books from Amazon, Barnes & Noble, Kobo, and Apple, so if you are using a third-party distributor to sell through these sites, you will have streamlined financial reports but will be losing out on royalties. It is up to you to weigh the pros and cons.

The Journey of the Self-Published Author and the E-Book

Karen McQuestion, author of the e-book *A Scattered Life*, has sold thirty-six thousand copies (and counting) directly through Amazon's Kindle store. After failing to garner attention from traditional publishers or agents, she decided to upload her novel to Amazon's Digital Text to drum up some attention—and it worked. "I thought, if nobody buys it, I can just take it down," said McQuestion in the *New York Times*. After ensuring her book's marketability and establishing a strong readership, *A Scattered Life* is now printed through Amazon and available in paperback.[10] Indie authors are a driving force behind the recent surge of e-book titles, with about 2.8 million self-published and micro niche titles produced in 2010, up 169 percent from 2009.[11]

E-books provide opportunities for unknown authors to break into the market with low risks and potentially high rewards. Some authors have found success using e-book publishing for marketing purposes, choosing to release portions of their books to tease and test the market. Other authors choose the e-book format as their only method of publishing. The trick to making the best choice for your book is examining your marketing plan and target audience. All genres aren't created equal in the e-book world. For instance, fiction is currently the top-selling genre for e-books; Book Industry Study Group (BISG) research shows that readers are less likely to use e-readers for textbooks, travel books, religious literature, young-adult literature, or for academic or professional purposes.[12] Consider if your book's genre is a good fit for an e-book and research what percentage of your target demographic owns an e-reading device. Several genres, such as reference, guide, technology, romance, and science fiction, have been doing well in the e-book arena for some time.[13] Author Robin Dedeker, who published her memoir as an e-book, explained:

What I've learned about having my book available as an e-book is that it's the way books should go first. Instead of trying to guess how many books you're going to sell, it's a great way to make your book available and connect with readers at any time of day. It gives you an opportunity to promote your book all the time. People I've reached were able to access my book in minutes because of it being an e-book.

Don't ignore Robin's point about convenience. The opportunity to have books reach audiences in record speed is why publishers like Harlequin have offered their romance novels electronically for years. With e-books, buyers satisfy their impulses more quickly and at a lower cost.

E-Book Marketing

Marketing your e-book is as important as marketing your printed book. Interestingly, while publishers have placed priority on the online presence of printed books, they have not marketed e-books with the same attention. Don't fall into this trap. If you opt to offer an e-book: terrific. However, make sure you direct traffic to the websites that offer it. Make it known through social media, events, and news media that your book is offered in an e-book format and publicize the purchase information. You might have to offer online newsletters, send out press releases, make online updates, or even think about print ads, just as you would with a printed book. I worked with one author who offered his e-book for free with the purchase of his printed book, thus making the e-book a marketing tool.

Benefits of E-Book Publishing:

- **Minimal production and distribution costs.** Where self-publishing a printed book costs thousands of dollars, publishing the same content in an e-book format would be well under a thousand dollars and may even be free. Don't forget, however, to engage a professional editor. A book in any format should be professionally edited before being published. When readers are overwhelmed with distracting errors (which the translation into e-book format is notorious for introducing), it can interfere with their perception of the book, no matter the quality of the content.

- **Limitless Accessibility.** E-books are easy to plug by word-of-mouth. Many e-reader devices offer a tool to review a book and post it immediately to the Internet. A happy consumer is able to send a link to a friend, who then purchases and downloads the book instantly.

- **Unlimited sales opportunity.** Once a book is an e-book, it is permanently available for purchase online and on e-readers. It will never go out of print.

- **No returns.** Period.

- **E-books are here to stay.** Electronic publishing will only get more and more advanced. Today's college students were born in the Internet era and don't remember computer-free life. E-books will only become more and more prominent as these generations (and e-book–reading devices) age. Authors of every generation should consider going digital to ensure their book's long-term potential.

- **E-book technology is not limited to the young.** Though new technologies are often lost on older generations, e-book readers are perfectly poised for success with older adults. Those with difficulty reading small text have limited options in print titles available in large type. E-readers can modify the font size to whatever is most comfortable. Some e-readers even read out loud with their "text-to-speech" option.

- **Authors benefit from consumers' luxury of instant gratification.** Authors will appreciate that their readers enjoy the instant gratification of buying e-books. Rather than taking the time to drive to the store or waiting for the book to ship, they can begin reading the book instantly from just about anywhere.

- **E-readers are not required for reading e-books**. People don't need e-readers to read e-books—they only need computers. E-book vendors have free PC and Mac software available for people who want to purchase e-books and read them. E-books are also accessible on all smart phones.

The Hallmarks of E-Book Publishing:

- **Authors are working harder to connect visually with their readers.** The allure of the book cover on screen isn't quite the same as it is in hardcopy. Because there is no physical book to hand directly to readers, authors are finding creative ways to connect so as not to completely lose the "visual" angle when marketing.

- **E-books are steadily priced lower than printed books.** Where a printed book might be $16.95, e-books on average have a cover price of $9.99, and to be competitive, many authors are even pricing their book at $0.99. However, new royalty models have been implemented by the major e-book sellers that give authors and publishers a larger piece of the pie.

- **Authors are increasingly Internet-savvy and marketing books online.** Because e-books function solely on technology (social media, search engine optimization, and direct online communication with audiences) Internet marketing is vital to the success of an e-book.

The most encouraging development is that e-book readers read more than traditional book readers.[14] This fact is good news for the publishing industry and especially good for authors. Making your book available in e-book format is a way to reach readers you might otherwise miss.

Helpful e-book publishing tips:

- If you're working with a publisher, inquire about their e-book production process, including their timeline, conversion methods, and quality checks.

- Don't skimp on editing and design. These are critical to the success of your e-book. An amateurish book won't be respected or shared and may even garner bad reviews.
- Proofread your e-book carefully for mistakes before and after the conversion from manuscript to ePub file. Hiring a professional proofreader is highly recommended.
- Become as engaged in online marketing as possible; while back-of-the-room sales may work best for printed books, e-books require the author to engage in online social media.

THE LAST WORD

- E-books are a booming industry with quickly evolving technologies, and they are becoming more popular and mainstream by the minute.
- Books available as e-books are not only reaching more readers, but *new* readers. With e-books, long-term opportunities for books abound.
- E-publishing reduces publishing costs and the time it takes to reach readers, but authors will need to be diligent marketers, as with a printed book.
- E-books offer permanent and endless profit potential.

 Indie Author Wisdom

"I say, publish your book as an e-book because you can, just as authors of long ago made the leap to publish their books in print using machines rather than hand scribe one copy at a time. The e-book is the next leg of the journey, so don't miss out!"

~Robin Dedeker, author of *Moments of Intuition*

PART III

MARKETING YOUR BOOK

*Think left and think right and think low
and think high. Oh, the thinks you
can think up if only you try!*

~Dr. Seuss, *Oh, the Thinks You Can Think!*

Marketing and Sales 101

When I asked authors to share the most challenging aspect of publishing, the response was almost unanimous: marketing. Marketing is by far considered the most time consuming and most difficult part of being an indie author, often requiring outside-the-box (and bookstore) thinking. Children's book author Patrick Mader agrees: "The marketing has the most challenges. It's hard work selling yourself, and I don't think many authors realize the marketing required—people who've written a book sometimes feel they're owed something, and this isn't the right attitude."

In my experience, I find marketing works better when it is approached as an ongoing process that begins the moment you decide to publish. Rachel Anderson, a marketing and PR consultant, shared, "The biggest marketing mistake many authors make is waiting until after the book is published to begin marketing it. Authors should really be taking marketing into consideration while they are writing the book, which is typically not the case."

Marketing is a discipline used by businesses to convert people's wants or needs into profitable opportunities. How's that for jargon? And what does this mean for you? Simply put, marketing is a tool to demonstrate to readers why your book is important. Savvy indie authors are the primary marketers for their books and should do the following:

- Learn your readers' needs.
- Learn your readers' wants and requirements to have their needs met.
- Shape your book so that it meets their needs.
- Inform your readers about *how* your book meets their needs.
- Persuade your readers that your book meets their needs better than other books.

Many authors believe marketing is about promotion, advertising, and sales when truly it's about consistency. Decide in the beginning how you want readers to perceive your book, and carry that through in all communication with them, including your website, business card, sell sheet, social media communication, and in the media. Frequently changing your message, voice, and mission hurts your credibility and makes you appear amateur. Additionally, successful authors must maintain a steady presence in the marketplace, even when it feels like no one is paying attention. Readers eventually notice books they come across multiple times. Don't be shy and don't give up.

Author DeAnne Sherman advised, "Tell your potential readers why your book is superior or special and what kernels of wisdom they'll get from reading it. Spread the word about what you have brought to your book to make it worth buying. Talk about your book as beautifully and assertively as you would someone else's book."

The marketing mantra in business is this: Marketing comes first, marketing drives the product, marketing drives the process, and marketing is king. As an individual launching a product into the marketplace, consider that more than 90 percent of products fail yearly. When it comes to publishing, one million books are published worldwide each year, with two hundred thousand produced in the United States alone. A book is published every thirty seconds. Competition is steep out there. Meeting your publishing goals is far from impossible, but if you think a book will sell itself, you're wrong. However, if you're hesitant about self-publishing based on marketing requirements, don't be. Much like writing and publishing, book marketing is simpler than you think if you're willing, flexible, and committed. Everything from contacting media, to setting up and attending book events, to simply telling a total stranger about your book is all marketing. Novelist Marilyn Jax explained,

> New books come out every day. Competition is fierce and relentless. It is up to you as the author to continue with an ever-present, non-stop rhythm of marketing. I always carry books to a restaurant and set them on my table. This usually gives me the opportunity to tell the server about my book and often people at surrounding tables, too. Likewise, I tote a few books along with me in my arms whenever I fly.

Marilyn's method of making sure her book has an "ever-present, nonstop rhythm of marketing" is as simple as being prepared at a moment's notice to promote her book. As an indie author, you'll find that these opportunities happen regularly and naturally—you just have to be ready to take advantage of them. Marilyn Jax continues, "Oftentimes, people on my flight have asked to buy a signed copy of one of my books. I have even had a flight attendant make an announcement over the intercom that I am on the flight and mention the titles of my books. Great advertising!" Being prepared to spread the word is step one. If you can do that, you'll become more comfortable in your role as a marketer in the long run.

Another secret I've heard from countless authors is to look where you least expect to sell your book. Author Colleen Baldrica found this to be true, "Once I thought outside the box and looked at alternative ways to market my book, doors opened. I recommend going to grocery stores. Don't just think bookstore. Create and attend events that aren't necessarily book events, like arts and crafts events." Ken Thurber, author of *Big Wave Surfing: Extreme Technology, Development, Management, Marketing & Investing,* approached marketing deliberately and aggressively, factoring outside-the-box opportunities like targeting small business bloggers. One author I worked with went to her local gym, which happened to belong to a big chain. They selected her book as a book club selection of the month, which drove an onslaught of buyers to bookstores and created appreciated buzz.

> **Once I thought outside the box and looked at alternative ways to market my book, doors opened. I recommend going to grocery stores. Don't just think bookstore. Create and attend events that aren't necessarily book events, like arts and crafts events.**

The Nuts and Bolts of Your Marketing Plan

If you're still wondering where to start, create a marketing plan. A marketing plan highlights methods for reaching readers and fosters confidence in bookstores that a book won't be sitting on the shelf without a strategy. It should be simple and straightforward. It doesn't have to be perfect, or even final. In fact, it will and should grow as you expand your reach. A corporate bookstore executive and buyer shared,

A Grassroots Marketing Lesson from John Grisham's Publisher

Back in 1991, when John Grisham was an unknown author, his publisher was confident that his books were good enough to reach the mass market. So they embarked on a marketing strategy that today would be considered extremely "grassroots." They referred to it as "hand selling." Rather than relying solely on good reviews to sell the book, they took to the streets, giving copies to bookstore clerks and encouraging word of mouth to spread[15]. It worked, and Grisham became a household name.

What should we learn from this? Even though you might not be able to send a sales force across the country, you should start locally by reserving a few of your book copies to give away to people who are willing to spread the word, starting with your local independent bookstore. Connecting with bloggers is also an effective grassroots marketing strategy.

We won't carry a book without a marketing plan. Many self-published authors make the mistake of not giving us a marketing plan, and we need that—even for the most perfect book. Without a marketing plan, we think the book isn't going to be promoted. Why would I put a book on our shelves if I don't think it has marketing support?

One word of advice: Remember your marketing plan is only that—your *plan*. Even if you haven't figured out specifics, write down every possible idea anyway. Retailers want to see that you're at least thinking about promotion and have plans in the pipeline. **Every marketing plan is different, but here are the nuts and bolts of what should be included:**

- **Book Specifications**: Include the basic details of your book: page count, trim size, ISBN, price, website address, and your contact information.
- **Book Cover Image**: Include a small picture of your front cover to give your marketing plan more flavor and help retailers and media remember it.
- **Book Synopsis**: Write a two-hundred-word summary of your book highlighting the important facts and identifying the problems that your book solves. For fiction, highlight the major conflict of the story without giving too much away. For nonfiction, include what's new, unique, helpful, entertaining, and distinctive about your book that affirms its value for readers.

- **Endorsements**: Quote credible sources that highlight your level of authority on the topic.
- **About the Author**: Summarize credentials relevant to your book that reinforce your authority.
- **Target Audiences**: Describe characteristics of your readers—by profession, background, experience, or interests, as well as by gender, age, race, or other relevant traits.
- **Upcoming Events and Signings**: List where you plan to promote your book. Highlight the geographic areas you intend to reach. Describe local opportunities in detail.
- **Media & Sales Contacts**: List persons, organizations, or resources you intend to contact about your book. Look for associations, organizations, and institutions to which your readers belong and list their contact information.
- **Awards and Contests**: Include ones you have either won or intend to enter in the next twelve to eighteen months.
- **Television and Radio**: List interviews you have had or are working on arranging.
- **Sales Methods**: Will you make cold calls? Do you have a list of warm calls to start with? How will you target of large groups? Name businesses, networking groups, and community-service organizations where you can give presentations or showcase your book.
  - Identify seasonal influences on book sales (both challenges and opportunities): Think three to four months ahead for publicity opportunities.

- How will you attract and keep readers?
  Describe the type of promotion and advertising you'll use: flyers, ads, postcards, e-mails,
  blogs, websites, etc.
- Describe any website or social media promo-
  tions: special offers, e-mail newsletters, etc.
- Will you offer credit to your customers? That
  is, how will you make it as easy as possible to
  buy your book directly from you? Does your
  website/publisher enable easy purchases and
  order fulfillment?

Hiring a Publicist

Have you ever wondered how an unknown author is suddenly a guest
on a popular morning or late-night talk show? Or how some books
have a long list of endorsements? A publicist is probably the answer.
Publicists are professionals who get your book in front of as many
people as possible and are known for their impressive repertoire of
prized contacts collected over many years. In the words of Rachel
Anderson, publicist and owner of RMA Publicity, "A publicist has
connections to the mainstream media and knowledge about what
they are looking for in a story. Find a publicist with media experience
and your chances of getting coverage go up astronomically."

Most often, publicists are go-getter types who go to bat for their
clients, relentlessly securing events, media coverage, speaking engagements, and endorsements. Gregg Proteaux, author of *Attitudes at Every
Altitude,* explained,

After a few months, I found I could not reach several channels on my own, so I worked with a local publicist who [secured appearances] on television programs, on radio programs, and at book signings that I could not have secured, including out-of-state events.

Over the years, I've worked with publicists who all have unique strengths and skills. One publicist I know was a news reporter for many years and has the ability to write articles on behalf of her clients and submit them to news publications. Another is gifted in event planning and sets up signings, launch events, and speaking engagements for her clients. My continuous advice for working with publicists is to hire them only for the tasks that you can't do yourself.

An attorney turned stay-at-home mom turned children's book author discovered she had the time and the ability to make calls to news stations, write press releases, and set up signings. She hired a publicist to focus on opportunities for national exposure because she was able to tap into the local market herself. Joining forces with a publicist should be a strategic partnership. Target a publicist who knows your audience well and will provide a blueprint for how to reach them.

Also, make sure your publicist reads your book! Some publicists rely on their clients to tell them what they need to know rather than reading the books for themselves. In order to pitch a book from every possible angle and speak about it confidently, a publicist has to read it. A well-known book reviewer confided in me that one of her biggest frustrations is being contacted by publicists who aren't knowledgeable about their clients' books. Ask your publicist how he or she feels about reading your book, and if there's any hesitation, consider it a warning sign.

Here's a checklist to follow *before* making the leap to hire a publicist:

- ☐ Set clear big-picture goals for what you want your publicist to accomplish (e.g. expand your national reach, create buzz for an upcoming event, grow your speaking platform).
- ☐ List each service you'd like a publicist to commit to (e.g. create a media kit, distribute press releases, secure TV and radio appearances, assist with a blogging tour, or solicit endorsements).
- ☐ Think of a small task to work on first, such as writing a press release or collecting endorsements, before launching the larger marketing campaign.
- ☐ Review the successes of prior campaigns before deciding on a publicist.

When it comes to working with a publicist, most authors want and request different things.

The most common question is "Can you help me sell millions of copies or get me in front of Oprah?" To that, Rachel Anderson said,

Maybe, but you have to be realistic. There's no secret formula. It's all about timing and luck. I came close to getting an author on the Oprah Winfrey Show once, but then my contact left the show, and her replacement wasn't as interested in the story I was pitching. Even without Oprah, we were still able to sell thousands of books on our own by working hard not just to reach the masses, but our target audience. That's pretty good for an unknown author.

Strategies for Creating Demand

While it sounds frightening, authors have to create their own demand and drive their book's success. Every author's methods for creating demand are different, and that's okay. Some authors create demand by pursuing as many speaking opportunities as possible. Some indie authors have created demand through the use of social media and have become experts at using sites like Twitter, Facebook, and LinkedIn. A large number of authors focus on shops, bookstore events, and regional markets. Patrick Mader, author of three children's books, shared,

> *"Being a teacher, I have the skills to present teachable moments to children. I include educational tools in my presentations and look for opportunities to engage my young readers. Also, because there's a spiritual component, in addition to libraries and schools, I approach vacation bible schools and women's groups. I also make a point to have props."*

What's comforting about creating your demand is that when it comes time to get out there, you'll have a clear understanding about your audience. Creating demand for your book does not have to be expensive and does not require paying a PR professional tons of cash—you can slowly create your demand. Deirdre Van Nest, author of *Fire Your Fear: How to Grow Your Business by Changing the Way You Think,* uses networking as a method for creating demand, explaining, "I belong to a weekly networking group and I use it to promote my business. I also make sure my book is visible." Networking is one of the most cost-effective ways to create awareness and have face time with read-

> **Networking is one of the most cost-effective ways to create awareness and have face time with readers, yet many authors don't count it as marketing.**

ers, yet many authors don't count it as marketing. Also, don't forget the power of publicity for speaking engagements. Children's author Patrick Mader shared, "Free publicity as a speaker can save hundreds of dollars when you consider advertising for the event, especially in print media."

Here are more strategies for creating demand at a low cost:

- **Gather contacts.** Create a list of possible media contacts, including contact information.
- **Organize your contacts.** Create a separate list of everyone you know who will support and buy the book. Make sure you send updates to this e-mail list, when you win a book award, when you schedule the time and place of your next appearance, or when your book is featured or mentioned by the media.
- **Create targeted pitch letters and press releases.** Send them to media outlets, your professional networks, and

your growing contact list regularly (see samples in the appendices).

- **Advertise.** If you intend to advertise, plan to have no less than six placements of your ad. Repetition is the trick that makes you more recognizable, but it takes time. Choose smaller newspapers, independent publications and blogs to keep your costs down. Goodreads and Facebook are also effective venues for ads.

- **Network.** Make a list of important places where you can network with possible buyers of your book.

- **Become a speaker.** Volunteer to speak at monthly luncheons for BNI groups, local Chamber of Commerce chapters, Lions clubs, Masons clubs, Rotary clubs, networking organizations, and other volunteer organizations.

- **Target libraries.** Talk to a librarian about local book clubs that might be interested in selecting your book.

- **Write articles.** Create articles that complement the subject matter in your book. Submit these to magazines, e-zines, and relevant newsletters. Include a quick tidbit about you and your book.

- **Create a blog around your book's topic.** Be creative, and have fun with your blog. It will help you connect with your readers and gradually build a platform. You'll have to be committed if you want a successful blog—post a minimum of once a week, otherwise your readers will probably grow restless waiting for updates. Don't forget to comment on other blogs, and include a link to yours.

- **Create an online newsletter.** Newsletters establish you as a credible expert and provide consistent access to your audience, building and expanding your fan base. Another plus: There's no daily or even weekly maintenance, as with a blog.

- **Use the Internet.** Network for free online. Add the web address for your book's website to the signature in every e-mail you send out. Join social-media sites like Twitter and Facebook to increase your visibility. To be successful, however, make sure you update or post regularly (at least once a week, if not more). Social medial communications dashboards such as Hootsuite (www.hootsuite.com) allow you to schedule updates in advance and monitor relevant activity.

- **Drop the name of your book**—and your own name—whenever possible. Be shameless about how sensational your book is. Talk to anyone and everyone about your book, because you never know who might turn out to be a valuable connection. Consider leaving your business card in a waiting room or putting a promotional book-mark in a library book you are returning.

Part of marketing in the publishing world is simply being alert and monitoring the marketplace. Is there a particular topic or trend that your book addresses? Is the marketplace asking a burning question or facing a particular problem that you have an answer to? Self-published authors have often been successful at capitalizing on a "hot" topic with substantial media coverage by paying attention to how their book connects to a current event or story in the news.

Creating demand locally is as simple as having "local author" stickers placed on books sold through your local bookstores. Locals usually love their homegrown talent and delight in supporting local authors. Don't neglect the events and independent bookstores right in your backyard. Local media outlets will be happy to feature your book signing or tie your book into a future news story.

Take your book to high school reunions and publicize it in alumnae publications. Much of your marketing efforts will be grassroots, meaning you'll start with your innermost circle and gradually expand outward. The Internet is a wonderful tool for quickly reaching broader networks outside that circle, but you'll discover that starting with your friends and family is an instant way to jumpstart the word-of-mouth buzz that's so important in the first year of a book's launch.

Redefining the Best Seller

I worked with an author who sold more than twenty thousand copies of his book in its first six months, and it became the best-selling sports book in his state. This was an incredible achievement—and I should add that this author sold

> Many authors dream of having a "best seller." Truthfully, your book may have that potential—you simply have to give thought to what "best seller" means for your book, in your genre, with your strengths, and your message.

more copies of this book than did the *New York Times* best sellers in his book's genre at the time. Many authors dream of having a "best seller." Truthfully, your book may have that potential—you simply

The Long Tail and Why You Should Care

The long tail is a phenomenon that indie authors know well. In 1988, a book entitled *Touching the Void* by Joe Simpson, a harrowing tale of near death in the Peruvian Andes, had moderate success. Ten years later, another book, *Into Thin Air* by Jon Krakauer, made it big. Amazon's "customers who bought this" referral tool propelled the ten-year-old book of related content onto the *New York Times* best-seller list for fourteen weeks because readers were interested enough in Krakauer's book to buy Simpson's book at the same time. The "Long Tail" phenomenon demonstrated the power of the Internet, and specifically the fact that Amazon can give books unlimited shelf lives.

Remember that your book, thanks to the Internet, has several "lives." It can dovetail with a national story that suddenly pops onto the radar, or with a movie that becomes the rage. Keep your eyes peeled for the day-to-day newsmakers, trends, and topics that have people talking and then connect them to your book! Two women I know co-authored an award-winning book on grief and managing loss and became quoted experts in the *New York Times* following the untimely deaths of several celebrities in a short time period. Even though their book was a few years old, they were able to have a fresh sales spurt because of the coverage.

have to give thought to what "best seller" means for your book, in your genre, with your strengths, and your message. A book can be a best seller without ever making it on the *New York Times* list. For the record, the *New York Times* determines their best-sellers list by tallying sales (not including returns) from select independent bookstores, chain bookstores, wholesalers, gift shops, newsstands, and supermarkets.[16] They keep the "stores list" confidential, and the stores on the list are also asked to "filter out" corporate sales (i.e., bulk sales to companies) that might appear to influence a book's best-seller potential.

The best-seller lists don't factor sales from price clubs, specialty stores, or bulk orders bought through organizations, even though books sales from nontraditional book outlets account for almost half of all books purchased in the United States.[17] My advice: Don't get hung up on trying to get on the best-seller lists.

If you're an indie author, the reality is that unless you figure out which stores are counted by the *New York Times*, print enough copies of your book to be carried across the country, and then launch a major marketing campaign to move those books, you'll probably not end up on the *New York Times* best-seller list. It's not unusual for self-published authors to sell in the thousands to nontraditional channels. Selling to nontraditional outlets is often better for authors overall. The profit potential is higher, and focusing on who needs your book the most is the best way to get your book in front of your prime audience. Pursuing alliances with channels outside of bookstores can result in your book becoming the "best-selling" book of your genre—without the *New York Times*.

THE LAST WORD

- Consider book marketing an ongoing process that has no right or wrong method and requires a dedicated amount of time to be effective.
- Indie authors are often shocked to find out that they have to create their own demand. The sooner you own this fact, the more successful you'll be at building a following.
- Indie authors' unanimous word of advice on marketing: Think outside the bookstore.

 Indie Author Wisdom

"I think the ongoing marketing and selling is challenging. The writing was easy. If I could go back, I would have had the marketing up and running before my book was released—that might have helped more."

~Derek Wolden, author of *Basketcases: How Youth Basketball Parents Can Lower Their Blood Pressure and Not Lose Their Sanity*

Chapter 11

Survival Secrets of Marketing, Publicity, and Book Events

Although there's no single answer or trick to book promotion, plenty of resources are at your fingertips to help get your book raveworthy buzz. As Marilyn Jax, author of three novels, put it,

I do a wide variety of author events, from book signings, readings, and discussions in bookstores to art fairs, speaking at community events and restaurants, and participating in neighborhood book groups. An eyeglasses company also sponsors me by advertising my books on the back of bookmarks sent out with all orders—nationally and internationally. All television and radio interviews are excellent sources of spreading the word as well. Finally, I hand out bookmarks advertising my mystery novels wherever I go.

As Marilyn shows, there are countless ways to promote your book. In our current market, your book displayed at bookstores won't cut it as your only method of promotion. Author Gregg Proteaux agreed:

> *I thought that once my book was published and on the shelf, it would sell itself! It just doesn't happen that way. A dear relative who is also very successful in business asked me "Why do you think Coca-Cola spends millions yearly on promotion?" My advice to authors is to [include] promotion in your budget.*

Gregg is spot on. Factor both the cost and time of book promotion. Especially time. You don't have to spend a fortune; there are several free and inexpensive ways to promote your book. But you've got to put in the time. And doing something—whether working with a publicist, connecting with media, or attending events—is always better than doing nothing.

Attracting the Media in the 21st Century

Before I knew much about the media, I thought reporters were impossible to reach and that pitching a story was unfeasible. I quickly learned that finding the right person wasn't hard. I also found that if a book is timely with a well-defined hook, reporters, radio show hosts, and producers are willing to do a story about it. Rules in the media world are changing every day. In the words of Laurie Hertzel, senior editor for the *Minneapolis StarTribune* and author of *News to Me: Adventures of an Accidental Journalist*, "Authors should do a little research to determine which editor is the right one to contact. Pitch your book to them in a short, professional e-mail. Don't gussy it up, and always include a peg."

You're probably wondering what the heck a "peg" is. Reporters are constantly seeking material for their next story, but authors who send books without addressing it to the proper person and with the appropriate pitch will never get a call back—it's in fact considered spam. Ouch! That hurts, but get used to the fact that your book's release is not considered news to the media. Books are more likely to receive attention when linked to a peg or a hook—something to connect your book to, such as a national news story, solution to a widespread dilemma, or a timely event.

For instance, one author (let's call her Anne) is a thought leader in the world of corporate ethics. Reporters frequently call Anne for comments whenever a major story breaks featuring a company's compromise of ethical codes since her books and successful training business have positioned her as the expert. Because reporters operate in a deadline-driven world where timing is everything, an indie author who does a little strategizing is well-positioned for such opportunities.

> **Books are more likely to receive attention when linked to a peg or a hook—something to connect your book to, such as a national news story, solution to a widespread dilemma, or a timely event.**

If, like Anne, your book can be used as a resource for a news story or featured in articles tied to the topic of the hour, it stands a good chance of getting noticed. If you don't hear back from someone, there's no harm in following up. I encourage it. A gentle reminder by e-mail is okay, but in the words of Laurie Hertzel, "Don't hound. Hounding isn't good. Our time is very valuable. If a book has a good pitch and we have some lead time, we'll get back to the author."

Here are my secrets for dealing with media—abide by these and you'll stay on their good side:

- **Don't send anything blind**: Send pitches, news releases, and announcements to the right person at the right publication. Sending to "Dear Business Reporter at…" or "To whom it may concern" is a big no-no.

- **Always pitch the solution**: Journalists want to know "What's in it for the audience?" Outline the ways your book solves a problem and why it's unique.

- **Do your research**: Doing some investigating will reveal the kinds of stories journalists look for, which empowers you to angle your pitch effectively.

- **Make it easy**: The less work a reporter has to do, the more likely they are to bite. Supply an engaging hook, significant statistics, a bio, and book specifications. If there's important information or details missing, they'll skip to the next thing.

- **Send an e-mail, not postal mail**: An e-mail is quick to respond to and the preferable method for being contacted. Even calling is sometimes viewed as a nuisance. Anything sent by postal mail will get lost or thrown away.

- **Don't send attachments**: Use the body of an e-mail to say what you want to say. Attachments from unknown senders are a bother and most are sent to the spam folder. Only send an attachment when asked.

News releases are a traditional method used by PR profession-als to attract media attention. Some authors use sites like PR Web and News Wire to distribute releases, while others rely on publicists to send releases on their behalf. The hope is that a reader, reporter, or important news outlet comes across the release and contacts the author for a story. In my world, releases are sent not only to media, but also to bookstores and bloggers as well. You'll need to think a little dif-ferently about news releases since word-of-mouth is the best way to get your book into the marketplace. A news release should read like an article with quotes, current statistics, and a hook to grab readers. Cre-ate several news releases that can be used for different purposes and keep creating them as new trends and national topics arise. The ideal circumstance is to not only attract media, but also to have your news releases reach bloggers and consumers online via search engines and RSS feeds.[18] Author Ken Thurber said,

When you send out a press release, you have to get someone to pick it up, so create an enticing headline. We worked hard at polishing our headlines to work to our advantage. Thanks to strong content and attention-grabbing headlines, I received 300 Google references from people who picked up our releases—news stations, bloggers, magazines, and sometimes even websites—scores of people. Hard-hitting headlines are the trick. You want a press release that's timely but that also stands out. Have a succinct message that's unique and different. If it's contro-versial, that's even better. News releases translate into sales, and you can track where those sales come from.

What Goes in Your Media Kit

First let's assume your media kit is electronic, i.e., on your author website. And let's assume that you're contemplating creating a media resources section or a "press room." Here's what you need:

1. **Downloadable cover art**
2. **Author bio**: Describe facts relevant to the audience of your book—your expertise, relevant work experience and titles, and accomplishments.
3. **Fact sheet or sell sheet**: State the facts about the book (title, author, publisher, number of pages, ISBN, publishing date, and price), ordering information, and has a brief synopsis of the book.
4. **Book milestones**: Include awards, accolades, book clubs, sales numbers, or anything that highlights a notable success.
5. **Questions and answers**
6. **Previous news releases**
7. **Pitches or "news pegs"**: List possible "angles" or "hooks" for a news story.
8. **Book testimonials and/or endorsements**
9. **Table of contents**
10. **Sample chapter**
11. **Interview clips**
12. **Media articles**
13. **Contact information/e-mail**

The Deal with Bookstore Events, Trade Shows, Festivals, and Conferences

Authors frequently ask me how involved they should be with bookstores and specifically how to navigate working with Barnes and Noble and online vendors like Amazon. Frankly, I believe that making your book available through both Amazon.com and big box bookstores is required if you want nationwide exposure. Selling your book is a process, and if you prepare yourself and plan ahead, scheduling out your events, signings, and appearances ahead of time, your books will move. But you have to be proactive.

Set reasonable sales goals, knowing which times of year are "hot" periods for your book. If you're a children's book author, you might find that the back-to-school season is best for sales and that you should concentrate your marketing efforts and goals to correspond with September and October. When you know your market, audience, and strengths, your goals will become more clear and focused. Another tip: Look at a bookstore's online events and see if you and your book complement any that are already scheduled.

> Another tip: Look at a bookstore's online events and see if you and your book complement any that are already scheduled.

Gary Mazzone, an event and sales manager for an independent bookstore said, "We're thrilled to help authors with bookstore signings, which raises a book's profile and gives it instant exposure." Event and sales managers like Gary Mazzone have seen it all and know how steep the competition is, so don't be shy about connecting with these managers and affirming your ability to bring traffic to their store. They'll often give helpful advice and clue you in about larger causes and future sales opportunities.

When you get your book in bookstores, book signings are an effective way to drive traffic to the store and also interact with your audience face-to-face. However, in truth, book signings are a mixed bag, since not all bookstores promote book signings, and many leave the author with the responsibility of bringing in the crowd. The trick to getting a bookstore to set up a signing for you is to convince them that your book is timely and well promoted. Bookstores get behind books that are worth their time. In the words of Gary Mazzone, outreach and sales manager for Magers & Quinn Booksellers:

> *The days of having several authors a month come in and sit at a table and sign books has changed. Readers are attracted to events that offer more than just a reading and an autographed book. Today's signings are multi-faceted and connected to larger events, causes, and trends that an author's book can be linked to. We're most interested in drawing a crowd, not just helping one author promote his book.*

Notify your contact list anytime you're going to do an event. This is especially important with a book signing. Preparing for a book signing involves more than listing upcoming signings on your website and expecting that someone else will spread the word. Send out an e-mail blast, make calls, and mention it to your networks. Many newspapers list local author and book events and oftentimes will do this for free, especially on their website. Book signings that are well promoted are well attended. If you're going to be on TV or radio, take that time also to promote any of your upcoming signings.

However, if you're at your book signing and it's not attracting lots of buyers, don't sweat it. You're out there and visible. Sign books and ask the bookstore if it will carry your book with "autographed copy" stickers on them; autographed books stand a greater chance of not being returned by bookstores. Derek Wolden, author of *Basketcases: How Youth Basketball Parents Can Lower Their Blood Pressure and Keep Their Sanity*, advised making book signings as interactive as possible: "If you're able to have events where you're actually reading for a part of it or there's a discussion, I think that works better. My readers are not the bookstore crowd, so book signings have been more random luck."

When preparing for your book signing, think about ways to spice it up and create outside-the-box interactions with your readers. **Here are a few ideas for ways to draw eyes—and hopefully more people—to your table:**

1. Have a standing sign displaying your book's cover, so buyers have a visual to draw them to the table.
2. Use bookmarks, props, candy, or balloons, create a fun atmosphere and attract visitors. Even a nice tablecloth goes a long way.
3. If a person is close by, kindly—and graciously—engage them in conversation.
4. If you have an e-book version, display it on your e-reader on the table.

When you have buyers at the table, add your own stamp to the event. A successful children's book author I've worked with brings her illustrator to as many signings, as possible. Together, they both sign books, and as a bonus, the illustrator sketches a quick picture below their autographs so the book becomes even more of a conversation piece and keepsake. She also gives away coloring pages and stickers of her characters to kids. An author of a cookbook has brought recipes with her to hand out as people walk by.

Have fun with your signings and add a personal touch. As author DeAnne Sherman said, "The glamour of book signings lasts about fifteen minutes, but you never know what will lead to something. There have been times I thought an event was a waste of time, and found out later that it led to a purchase of a hundred books."

Similarly, to be effective at trade shows, conferences, and festivals, authors have to stand out in the crowd. As an exhibitor at a conference or trade show, you're one of many, so you'll need to work the room, attract readers to your table, and network with other contacts who might be there. The biggest bonus of trade shows and conferences are the direct sales, so you want to make the most of them. **Here are my golden rules for scoring big at trade shows:**

- **Set goals for yourself.** Are you there to partner with an organization? Become a keynote speaker for the following year? Sell a certain number of books?
- **Dress the part.** Make an impression with your choice of dress. If you're a business book author, dress like one. If you're a children's book author, have fun with your clothing. One children's book author wears overalls since his book is about the farm; another wears a hat with a plush toy of her main character attached to it.

- **Be Prepared**. Research the other exhibitors who will be there and plan to make the rounds and introduce yourself to important players—bring business cards and a sell sheet to leave behind.
- **Be flexible**. If a chance or spontaneous meeting takes you away from your table, don't sweat it. The point of such events is to connect with buyers, and meet important contacts and potential mentors.
- **Follow up**. Don't promise to stay in touch if you don't really mean it or plan to follow through. Don't wait more than a week to follow up—keep the momentum going by staying fresh in the minds of good leads.
- **Stand**. One word of advice I'll always remember comes from my publishing mentor, Milt Adams, who says, "Don't be caught sitting at your exhibit table." Standing shows your passersby that you're ready to engage. Sitting sends the wrong message.

 ## What's Your Hook?

Let's say you're on the phone with a producer of a talk show interested in your book. What would you say when asked to explain what your book is about? If you pause, fumble, take too long a breath, or even sound remotely unsure, the producer will quickly move on to the next author, celebrity, or publicist. This is why every author needs a hook they can be confident in. What is a hook, exactly? Plainly, it's a provacative summary of your book that would capture a captivating news, talk, or radio show segment. How will you spin your book's message to prompt a knee-jerk reaction? One of my favorite hooks is from Suzanne Ruff, author of *The Reluctant Donor*. If you ask her what her book is about, she'll tell you, "It's about how terrified I was to donate my kidney to a sister I couldn't stand." Certainly her book is about much more than that, but her quick three-second hook raises eyebrows and evokes curiosity.

Here are a few things to keep in mind when coming up with your hook:

1. Find something new and different about your topic that makes your book stand out from the countless others competing for media coverage.
2. Your hook should be a concise, attention-grabbing sentence or phrase. If you take fifteen minutes to pitch your hook, start over.
3. Consider your background and personal story as a hook. Think J. K. Rowling writing *Harry Potter and the Philosopher's Stone* as a struggling single mother on welfare.
4. Your hook is also known as your elevator pitch. If you find yourself in an elevator with an influential person, say Oprah Winfrey, and you've got just a few moments to pitch your book and get her attention before the doors open, what will you say?

Your hook should give an audience with a short attention span a reason to remember you and go out and buy your book. If your book solves a problem, highlight that. If your fiction or even nonfiction book tells a compelling story, find a creative twist in that story with which to "hook" your audience immediately! General rule: Give them something to talk about.

The Art of the Book Launch

Throwing a book launch party is an explosive approach to sell directly to your audience right off the bat. After helping a few authors with their book launch parties, I've realized that a launch event of some kind is a must. Of all the book launch parties that I've participated in, there's never been one that didn't successfully jumpstart the book. Not only is a book launch party a chance to celebrate your hard work, but it also squelches that "What am I doing?" mindset. It's an author's debut party, and a crucial step in the journey of owning your authorship status. Book launch parties create buzz, jump-start sales, and offer a fun way to start marketing. **Here are some tips for planning a successful book launch:**

1. **Create an event:** Whether your event is at a bookstore or elsewhere, don't expect the crowd to come to you. Send out invitations. Inform your colleagues, friends, relatives, and everyone in your acquaintances circle about your book's coming-out party. Oftentimes, consumers are drawn to a crowd. Pardon the overused quote, but if you build it, they will come. Attract a crowd to you, and that

will probably bring in more of a crowd. Have food, music, and activities ready.

2. **Think outside the box**: If your book is a cookbook, set up a demonstration of your recipes at your party. One children's book author brought cake, coloring pages, and stickers to her book launch party for her little readers. It was a nice touch, and the parents took notice and gladly spread the word about her fun book and the ingenious method of engaging children. Decorate your table or venue to correspond with your book topic. Figure out ways to entertain your guests, even if it's something as simple as wearing an outfit that connects to the book. One author wore a custom-made baseball uniform to events to promote his biography of a baseball player from the early 1900s. It created quite the conversation!

3. **Enlist help**: Don't spend time at your launch party selling your book. Enjoy yourself! You are the guest of honor! Have a manned table of volunteers with an arrangement of books in a visible location where guests can buy a copy (usually at a discounted cost). As the author, you should be among the crowd, sharing your time and excitement with the people who've come to congratulate and support you.

4. **Choose your venue carefully**: A bookstore is an okay choice and will work if your event is advertised well and draws a crowd (see suggestion number one). However, restaurants work well, too. Guests tend to be in a good mood where there's food and drink, and they'll prob-

ably buy not just one book, but several. Grocery stores also work well. Grocery stores have a lot of traffic, and it's a prime location for authors of books with a local or regional focus to connect with their audience. One author had her signing at a newly opened consignment boutique. It was a nontraditional venue, but the store was thrilled with the opportunity to spread the word about their opening and promoted the author's event in return.

Essentially, when it comes to your launch party, make a splash. There's no need to spend much money—or even any. I advise authors to keep their costs as low as possible. The focus should be on getting your supporting networks involved with helping you spread the word about your book. Your book launch is simply that: a launch. It's a powerful beginning and the push you need to keep the momentum going.

Partnering with Libraries

Libraries attract a broad spectrum of patrons, offer free events, and serve the public, making them excellent avenues for giving presentations. Patrick Mader, author of the Opa and Oma children's series, focuses a large portion of his marketing on getting into library systems all over his state and region. With increasing momentum, his efforts snowballed into a thirteen-library contract, which includes speaking fees, gas money, and the opportunity to sell his book at almost every library event he now spearheads. His books are found in over two hundred libraries nationwide.

When I asked him a few questions about getting books in the library system, he provided insightful advice and tips. From his experience and others, I know that successful presentations lead to librarians recommending authors to other branch libraries within their regional system. It's likely that you'll get an "audition" at a library to prove that your book merits attention. If given this opportunity, prepare by bringing props and an engaging program that will appeal to wide-ranging audiences. Be enthusiastic and confident. It will show your credibility and, in turn increase their confidence in you and your book. **Here are more tips for getting your book in libraries:**

- Determine which libraries are a good fit based on the types of programs they promote and which speakers they invite to present.
- Research upcoming theme months and special events that your book might complement. (Use this strategy for bookstores as well.) Coordinate your efforts with holidays, National XYZ Month, movie releases, and local history events.
- Prepare by getting advice from other library performers, librarians, and patrons who you believe will offer an honest appraisal of your talents and message.
- Write a cover letter, and create a brochure that will appeal to the library's program director. Include something unique or an idea with a new angle; libraries want to offer something different.

- Practice your presentation. Hone it at other venues where you may already have an engagement. Post testimonials or references on your website.
- Know what materials you'll need (if any).
- Consider the questions you may be asked and be prepared with detailed answers.
- If you're a children's book author, request a side-sewn binding or "library binding" from your printer; this is considered the standard binding for libraries.

Libraries don't have the budget for presentations that are ill prepared or lack appeal. If you have no track record, you'll need to inform them of important points, your book's storyline, and which audience will best be served. If you land a program, be collaborative and prompt. Thank the audience for attending. Acknowledge them, and express your appreciation. Send the library staff a thank-you card afterward. It all creates goodwill and opens opportunities for the future.

Making the Most of Reviews and Testimonials

Testimonials and reviews are important assets throughout your book promotion efforts. As book marketing expert Sara Lien put it, "Book reviews are similar to endorsements. They are important, because they will give the book visibility online and in trade magazines. If a reader searches for a new author online and has a positive review come up, they will put more faith in that author." Media outlets like to know that your book has been well received. You might even consider providing an e-mail address on the author bio page of your book. Readers are sometimes so moved after reading a book that they'll send the author an e-mail, sharing their reading experiences. In fact, author Deirdre Van Nest shared, "As a speaker and coach, I get instant feedback on how I've helped clients. I've had readers call and e-mail me about how much I've helped them, and that's been rewarding—to see that I've helped readers without my even being physically present." In a case like Deirdre's, I advise taking advantage of those moving testimonials. If you have positive feedback about your business that your book complements, use those testimonials in your book as well. They show that you provide good results. If your book attracts comments from readers after it's published, place them on your website. Also use positive reviews in marketing materials such as postcards, sell sheets, and media kits.

Reviews also lead to media opportunities. In the words of book marketing guru John Kremer, author of *1001 Ways to Market Your Book*, "Any review is a good review." The idea is that both a good review and a bad review incite curiosity in the reader. You would be surprised which books became hits with bad reviews. Take the blockbuster *The Da Vinci Code,* which was eventually made into a major motion picture, and *The Shack,* which has sold millions of copies worldwide. Both books received a fair share of negative response from readers and reviewers and yet are publishing success stories.

Applying for Book Awards

One of the best things for your book is awards. Winning an award is a stamp of approval that adds credibility to your book and brings new life to the marketing process after a book's release. "Sally Brooks, author of *My Life: A Really Great Story*," sounds fine. But "Sally Brooks, author of the award-winning book *My Life: A Really Great Story*," sounds even better, and in the mind of a reader, an awarded book must be good. Authors who have won awards should take that opportunity to send out press releases highlighting their book's latest achievement, which results in news stories. Award winners typically receive stickers to attach to their books, which draw attention to the book and help it stand out from the competition. When you reprint your book, add the graphic image of the award seal on the front, and mention the award on the back cover.

The Rules of Following Up

How often have you exchanged business cards with someone only to never hear from them? Marketing your book is all about following up with prospective customers and connecting with people who expand your reach. Publicist Rachel Anderson advised,

> *My tip for getting book publicity is follow up, follow up, follow up. Whether you're reaching out to the media to secure a story or interview, a book store to set up a signing, or an organization to set up a speaking event, you need to follow up regularly until you get an answer.*

If you're not the best at following up, you'll need to get past that. It's not the easiest thing to follow up on every contact but I guarantee you'll be rewarded for your effort. Author DeAnne Sherman cautioned, "One of the biggest challenges is following up. We've made so many amazing contacts, but the follow up is hard because it's time-intensive, and you have to keep track of everything. Organization is key." DeAnne is right. It is hard to keep track of every contact. I suggest using a three-part contact strategy for the most important leads while maintaining a boilerplate e-mail or letter to send to multiple contacts that are the far-off leads (see the appendix for a boilerplate e-mail/letter sample). My three-part strategy for interacting with important leads is this: First, connect with your contact by phone or e-mail; second, send your information or forward your request; and third, follow up to ensure that your contact has received the request or information. A mistake authors frequently make is allowing opportunities to fall through the cracks. For example, many authors who go to trade shows or conferences spend the entire time at their table, hoping buyers will approach them.

> First, connect with your contact by phone or e-mail; second, send your information or forward your request; and third, follow up to ensure that your contact has received the request or information.

They're missing out. I know several authors who walk away with wonderful contacts at trade shows because they mingled with the crowd, exhibitors, and speakers. However, these contacts might not have led anywhere if these authors had not followed up with every single one, sent a book or sell sheet, and ensured that their connection led to a sale, other contacts, or both. If you're given the business card of a good contact, follow up with an e-mail referencing your last conversation. If you send an e-mail as your first interaction with a new contact, follow up with a phone call. People are busy and often appreciate a gentle reminder after you've made the initial connection with them. Authors often expect a barrage of immediate responses after they make initial contact, not realizing that folks in the publishing and media industry are bombarded with such materials on a regular basis.

If you have an online presence—and I hope you do—complete strangers will probably contact you about your book. Whether you get a negative, positive, or indifferent response, always take the time to reply to readers and reviewers. Readers often reach out to authors, especially ones who are local. Take that opportunity to communicate with them and foster relationships. Engaging in conversation with your readers (even if the communication occurs entirely online) places you on a more personal level with them. Be accessible, because interaction with readers leads to recommendations. If you intend to use social media as a means to market your book, responding to blog comments and queries through sites such as Facebook and Twitter will also help you build a following.

Keep every contact name and phone number in one place. If you're going to promote your book or book events electronically, a handy and growing list of names and e-mail addresses will prove particularly useful. Create a log that tracks your "base" contacts—these are readers, supporters, friends, family, and colleagues. This list will grow as you become more visible to the public as a published author. Your e-newsletters, blog posts, and frequent updates go to those on this list. Your base contacts

Your base contacts are your foot soldiers who want to spread the word and support your book.

are your foot soldiers who want to spread the word and support your book. Separate your sales leads from your base contacts. Sales leads include anyone in the media, organizations or corporate sales contacts, and retailers. Your sales leads list should be reserved for people with whom you'd want more strategic and targeted interaction with. Keep a log of every interaction with your sales leads list, and truly only contact them with a defined purpose in mind, such as featuring your book for XYZ Month in a publication or inquiring about a specific opportunity they have access to. There is danger in coming across as a nuisance to the contacts on your sales leads list, so you want to be careful with how frequently you reach out.

The Do's and Don'ts of Following Up

- Proofread all correspondence before sending or e-mailing.
- Don't use jargon, slang, or informal e-mail wording/emoticons (k, lol, or ☺).
- Call first if you intend to send an e-mail with an attachment.
- Be punctual if you set a date/time to follow up with a contact.
- If someone refers you to a good contact, send them a thank-you note or small gift.
- If a contact leads to a sales opportunity of any kind, short or long term, send a thank you note or small gift.
- Never leave the next date of contact open-ended; end with "I look forward to following up a month from now" or "When would you prefer I contact you again?"

Being Smart with Your Complimentary Copies

A word to the wise: be strategic with your complimentary copies, which are the copies you intend to give away. It's completely understandable that, once your book is finally in print, you'll want to scream from the rooftops, "It's here!" But keep in mind that it may not be wise to give most of your complimentary copies to friends and relatives. You need them to *buy* your book! Certainly keep a few copies for your personal stash. Authors often give away too many copies of their books, not realizing that they'll need a number of books to give away for promotional purposes.

It's a good idea, for example, to donate copies to museums and libraries, since they will often place orders based on their reviews of complimentary copies. In one case, a city's historical society loved a complimentary copy of a book that photographically conveyed the beauty of the city. They loved it so much that they bought all of the author's copies and even covered the second printing. Performance coach and author Deirdre Van Nest shared, "I always give at least one book away at speaking engagements."

Use your complimentary copies for the following:

- Pitching to media.
- Building a rapport with a contact that would lead to book sales, such as event coordinators for tradeshows and conferences, libraries, museums, or independent bookstores.
- As a gift to nonprofit organizations that might use or promote your book as a resource.

- As a raffle prize or giveaway at speaking engagements, conferences, or tradeshows.

Reaching Out to Your Readers

You'll certainly profit more from selling directly to readers than through other venues. As a self-published author, you make the full list price of your book—or close to it—when you sell directly to your readers. Author and performance coach Deirdre Van Nest stated, "I find direct-to-reader events great venues for connecting a name with a face, gaining exposure, and connecting with my audience in a fun way. As a self-published author, I think it's one of the best ways to promote my book."

The ugly truth is that selling your print book through Amazon and bookstores cuts your profit by more than half. Will it take effort selling directly to readers? Yes. Is it time consuming? Absolutely. It takes time to go to expos, trade shows, book festivals, and other events. Yet, these events are first-rate exposure and place you face-to-face with readers. These events are also great opportunities to network and build relationships with important people in the industry, including other authors.

I've heard countless stories about how authors got their "break" at a publishing event by talking to readers, agents, publishers, and other authors. At such direct-to-reader events, authors can pick up valuable information that leads to speaking gigs and other promotional opportunities. In his article "How a Self-Published Author Scored a Big New York Publisher," Bryan Chick explained that he beat his ten-thousand-copies sales goal by doing author visits to more than seventy schools. That combined with good word of mouth helped him sell twelve thousand copies of his children's book, *The Secret Zoo: Secrets and Shadows.*[19]

I advise authors to always carry copies of their books. Keep them in the trunk of your car, readily available for any sales opportunity. One author had books ready on the fly when the bookstore ran out of books at her first book signing. She had done her job promoting the signing, so she had a full house on the day of the event. In fact, so many people were at her signing that the store's supply of books was gone within the first hour. On the spot, this author was able to sell the books she had in her trunk. She then sold directly to authors *and* to the bookstore at a much lower discount because of the pinch they were in. Not only did she make more on her book than anticipated by simply being prepared with backup copies, but she also avoided the potential loss of business.

Once the book is published, and even after it's been in the market for a while, you'll need to keep your audience engaged. Through blogging, e-newsletters, social media, and sending simple e-mail updates to your growing contact list, pursue every opportunity to keep your book on readers' minds. Keeping readers engaged is also a keen way to develop a working list of frequently asked questions, increasing your credibility as a source of good information.

Word of mouth is a priceless and powerful marketing tool. How often have you researched someone based solely on hearing about it from someone else? **Here are a few tips to draw in readers:**

- Create a sweepstakes using social media. An example would be offering a signed copy of your book as a prize to the 100th person to "like" you on Facebook or send you a Tweet related to your book topic.

- Go to the blogs of potential readers and offer to guest blog.
- For any reader who reaches out to you personally, gather his or her contact information and send a personal note.
- Publicize your willingness to participate in any book club discussions on your book—even if it's out of state. Consider participating by phone or using a video conference technology like Skype (www.skype.com).

Involving Family and Friends and Making New Ones

Successful indie authors optimize their resources. Frankly, your greatest resource is your friends and family. They are your biggest fans and are usually happy to spread the word about your book. If your book is already published, keep them in the loop about your upcoming events and accomplishments. Most people are completely tickled to know an author and find it incredible that you've written and published your own book.

Also know that certain key people such as bookstore managers, members of associations affiliated with your book's topic, other writers, bloggers, and local library staff are allies too. Make an effort to introduce yourself to local bookstores and join publishing organizations in your area. Research writers' groups, and consider joining them. Being well-connected to the book world will offer access to valuable selling opportunities and expand your network, which is crucial to your success as an indie author.

THE LAST WORD

- When you think promotion, think persistence.
- Keep organized as you continue to promote your book. Keep track of your contacts, readers, and leads, and pay attention to trends. This will help you spot untapped channels and generate fresh marketing ideas.
- Try to send your materials to the appropriate people, addressed by name if possible. Don't forget to follow up!
- Out of marketing ideas? Make yourself a promise to tell at least three new people a day about your book. If you're still drawing a blank, books like John Kremer's *1001 Ways to Market Your Book* will generate fresh ideas.

 Indie Author Wisdom

"My unique strategies for promoting the book are thinking outside the box. This is essential when it comes to marketing. An author must target his or her audience. I am part of a group of award-winning authors that meets regularly to discuss what is working and what is not working as far as successful book marketing. The members of the group also plan functions where we all appear together at an event and mingle with people to discuss, promote, and sell our books. Between us, we offer a wide variety of genres: mystery; health and wellness; body, mind and spirit; and children's books."

~Marilyn Jax, author of *The Find, Road to Omalos* and *Sapphire Trails*

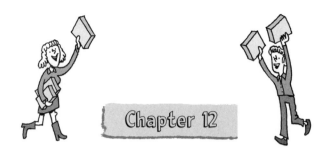

Sell Your Book Using the Web and Social Media

Consumers' comfort with the Internet creates an advantage for indie authors. Keep in mind that Internet book sales don't mysteriously happen: they take work. However, you won't find a more powerful marketing tool that allows you to build and grow your brand in engaging ways. When marketing your self-published book, there's no real magic bullet. Successful marketing has everything to do with building relationships, which is what the Internet is all about. Good marketing involves getting your book in front of as many people as possible. The Internet allows you do that with a website, blogging, online bookstore sites, electronic newsletters, and social media.

It's hard to imagine any person denying the Internet as an author's greatest ally. Yet I still come across a surprising number of authors who view the web suspiciously or see it as an extra step rather than an integral platform. My advice: View the Internet as a valuable tool—not an overwhelming challenge to overcome. It is the most cost-effective tool to generate buzz, and buzz sells books. The Internet saves time, money, and gas through every step of the publishing process, including writing, research, marketing, sales, and distribution. A well-designed author website creates a home base where virtually anyone can find you, expanding the audience far beyond what local marketing could do. Suzanne Ruff, author of the highly praised memoir *The Reluctant Donor* said,

> *A website is a must for your book. One of the most unexpected gifts of the web is how it helps readers contact me. Amazon allows readers to leave reviews. I've had great luck with Facebook—a cousin who lives in the Caymans whom I hadn't seen in years started a campaign on Facebook and played a huge part in helping me sell books.*

Authors become accessible to readers through the web, and that's what you want. "People investigate my website often," explained Patrick Mader, who wrote the Opa and Oma series. "People who buy my book usually have found my website first. It's standard for buyers to ask if I have a website. I think it's because they can find what they need without having to hear a sales pitch." As someone who works with authors, I'm impressed when I'm able to research an author online before working with them. In fact, it isn't unusual for agents, editors, bookstore personnel, journalists, and producers to Google an author's name while being pitched a book over the phone. Your book should have a visible presence on the Internet, but as an author, you should be a focus, too. Your web presence as an author coincides with your platform, so make sure that your voice shines through.

Create a Facebook page and Twitter account, participate in webinars, and post promotional videos on YouTube. This will expand your reach—and is well worth the effort that prompts too many authors to put a web presence on the back burner. Every business card, postcard, sell sheet, and even e-mail signature should point to your book's website and any social media accounts you have (Twitter, Facebook, LinkedIn, and YouTube). If you're on the web, readers will find you—it's that simple.

Creating Your Author Website

Authors should ultimately strive to have a website dedicated to their books, but as I mentioned, a focus on the book's platform is equally important. If you're new to the world of creating websites, not to worry; companies like Go Daddy (www.godaddy.com) and Word-Press (www.WordPress.com) offer site-building technology that take you through the process step-by-step.

If you have the means to hire a company or designer/developer to create a website, by all means go for it. A well-designed website shows that you're a professional. Let someone else focus on the technological side of things while you work on creating dynamic content. Many authors use a website simply for selling and marketing their books, which is fine, but the idea should be to keep your readers returning to your website frequently. You achieve this by updating your website with new content regularly.

One successful method for attracting repeat visitors is through creating a blog where you post new material on a consistent schedule. If readers enjoy your voice and know that you post every Wednesday,

Quick Facts on Internet Trends

- Most consumers research products using the web.
- Most book buyers know what book they're going to buy when they enter a bookstore, whereas online book buyers are more impulsive.
- Internet marketing is the biggest part of every publisher's marketing plan.
- The trick to a successful website is creating relationships with your visitors, NOT scoring one-time sales.
- The Internet should incorporate your book's brand by using your company logo, slogan, and your book's design.

they're more likely to check back weekly rather than once in awhile. An online monthly newsletter is another way to draw consistent traffic to your website. Be realistic about the time and effort you can reasonably contribute to the maintenance of your website, but make it a priority to keep it fresh and interesting. Even adding photos periodically will interest readers who return to your site. Dedicate one to two hours monthly, or at least quarterly, to refreshing your website content. Here's a tip: Hire an intern a few times a year to help with webpage updates, Twitter updates, blogs, and refreshing your e-mail contact list. You'll need to provide them strong direction, but it's worth it to delegate these tasks once in awhile, especially if you're busy with other aspects of your book.

Author Tim Munkeby's website homepage

If you plan to launch your website before the book is published—and you should—make sure your website's address is on your book to drive traffic to it. If you don't have immediate plans for a website, buy a domain name anyway and put it on your book. Of course, follow through on the endeavor, and don't abandon the idea.

Keep in mind that most interested consumers automatically assume all products have a website. Your website should educate the visitor about your book and why they should want to read it. Your website should also strive to connect them with your purpose and passion for your book's subject. Have fun with your website. Have a cover image placed on the homepage, but also put a photo of yourself on the "About the Author" page. Share your favorite links and create a photo gallery with images of you interacting with readers at various events.

Tips and Tools for Creating a Winning Author Website

- As soon as you settle on a title for your book, secure that domain name immediately.
- Keep your URL short. If your book title is long, consider using keywords or your first and last name in the URL; the latter option is especially beneficial if you intend to have multiple books or projects.
- Choose a URL that is memorable and easy to spell.
- Explain on your homepage what your book is about and list the key selling points.
- Include an image of your book's cover on the homepage.
- Offer the opportunity for a reader to buy directly through the website.
- Request that your website has a content management system built into it, which allows you to make updates to page content.
- Prior to meeting with a designer, make a list of websites that appeal to you.
- Provide an outline of all the features you'd like built into your site.
- Check website samples before hiring a website designer.
- Display your name and book title on every page within your website.
- Hire an expert to optimize your site for search engines.

Must-Haves for Every Author Website

- **All about you.** Somewhere on your site—whether it's the homepage or an "About Me" page—should be a bio that tells media and readers who you are.
- **Your contact information.** Don't forget to tell people how to contact you. If the content on your site appeals to a reporter or buyer but they can't easily find your contact information, you'll end up with one less contact that could potentially be important. An e-mail address or e-mail form is the minimum you should provide.
- **A picture of you.** While not obligatory, a photo is a nice touch to include on your site. Remember, you are part of the package!
- **A press page.** A press page makes it easy for the media to spread the word about you and your product. Include a downloadable PDF of the cover, press release, and sell sheet.
- **Testimonials.** Testimonials and reviews increase your credibility. Include any testimonials from editors, writers, or experts who reviewed your book. Also keep track of and post any positive feedback from readers.
- **Samples of your work.** To pique the media and readers' interest, include sample chapters, your table of contents, or clips of articles. Offer excerpts in different ways: as text on your site, as downloadable PDFs, Microsoft Word files, or as a password-protected document.
- **Buying 411.** Offer a method for immediate sales, whether it's through a form on your site or a link to your book's page on Amazon.com.
- **Personality.** Allow your personality to shine on your website.

Getting Google Savvy

Google continues to climb the ranks as the ruler of all things web, and today, web searching has become as intuitive as dialing a phone number. As an author, you have a few ways to make Google work for you. The most important way to ensure that people find your author website is to ensure that search engines give it priority. Search engine optimization (SEO to those in the know) is what enables search engines like Google to find and rank your site in their search results. Author Patrick Mader shared, "When people search 'heartwarming stories' on Google, my website is listed in the search results, which reinforces my niche." In Patrick's case, he's identified his book's niche as being "heartwarming stories about the heartland," and Google has indexed his website according to those keywords. The Google website provides suggestions for ways users can optimize their websites. One suggestion is using a significant word to your service or product (in this case, your book) in the URL that will help users remember and link to your site.

> **Google Alerts enables users to flag words or phrases of interest that Google will then monitor for you; it will send an "alert" with a link to any website with news or updates related to your word or phrase.**

One of my favorite Google tools for authors is Google Alerts, which helps you stay in the loop. Google Alerts enables users to flag words or phrases of interest that Google will then monitor for you; it will send an "alert" with a link to any website with news or updates related to your word or phrase. If your book is about sightseeing in Paris, you could set "tourists in Paris," "travel to Paris," and "vacation

Paris" as Google Alerts phrases. Google will flag any news story, blog post, or website that updates information with these words and e-mail a notice to you as often as you like: daily, weekly, or monthly. Google Alerts keeps you informed by flagging trends, your book title, and contacts in your subject area—all fresh information to promote your book.

These search queries save you valuable time and energy by combing the web regularly on your behalf. Here's a tip: Use Google Alerts to track how often Google catalogs your book title, website, blog, and social networking sites—this allows you to monitor your online presence. Here are some other tips to use Google to your advantage:

1. **Google's "I'm Feeling Lucky":** Use the most common keyword associated with your book, then click "I'm Feeling Lucky." It'll show you the most visited site using that keyword.

2. **Google Groups:** Search your book's topic, genre, or subject in Google Groups, which indexes millions of groups and forums by category. If interested, join any of them as a means to establish yourself as an authority, research your topic, or promote your book.

3. **Google Analytics:** A free service that tracks website traffic, number of page views, the location of visitors, and the most popular pages visited.

4. **Google AdWords:** If you're contemplating advertising your book online, Google Adwords is the place to start. It allows you to choose keywords, phrases, and subjects related to your book ad while also programming them

to show in select areas, with a specified budget. Google AdWords campaigns also link to Google Analytics, allowing you to monitor the traffic directed to your site from the ads.

5. **Google Docs:** Save your files to Google Docs and access your file on any computer anytime. As a part of Google's cloud-based office suite, Google Docs has editing capabilities, spell check, and sharing options. It is currently the best option for synchronizing a document across multiple platforms, including your mobile phone.

Amazon.com: Friend or Foe?

Amazon.com is a prime venue for your book and won't be losing momentum anytime soon. However, the challenge with Amazon is the 55 percent discount off the list price of your book, coupled with the guarantee that your book will be sold for less than your list price. You need to decide if the exposure and legitimacy of Amazon is worth the possible loss in sales. Some authors choose not to list their books with Amazon.

If you decide to list your book with Amazon, monitor the price of your book and relentlessly match or beat Amazon's price both when selling books directly to readers and also on your website. Amazon's exposure is a powerful tool to attract readers and get your book out there. The reviews of your book alone will help sell the book, not to mention the battalions of readers who research books on Amazon and then shop elsewhere. However, pocketing an entire sale, even if it is lower than your original asking price, is often more attractive than forfeiting hard-earned profit to Amazon.com. Ultimately I feel that, whether you like Amazon or not, your book will ultimately end up on Amazon.com because buyers can—and often do—resell their used books. It's possible that a reader or bookstore owner will purchase your book and turn around and sell it on Amazon.com.

Here are valuable tips to navigate Amazon.com's waters:

1. **Join Amazon.com's Author Central:** A free service that enables authors to reach more readers and promote their books. Creating an Author Central account gives your readers access to the "Search Inside the Book" function as well as to Kindle versions of your book.

2. **Use the Search Inside the Book program:** Allows readers to preview your book with a few sample pages of the interior and cover.

3. **Use your Amazon reviews:** When a reader or reviewer passes along their rave reviews, encourage them to post them on your Amazon.com book page. Research shows that the majority of consumers are more likely to make purchases after evaluating the reviews.

How to Use Facebook, Twitter, and LinkedIn to Grow a Platform

Social media is my absolute favorite Internet tool for authors. It's everywhere, and politicians, TV personalities, and celebrities all take advantage of the opportunity to interact with fans and supporters. I respectfully disagree with experts who advise using social media *only* if your customers use social media sites. If you're selling anything, you

Using Amazon's "Search Inside" Program

If you're an author with your book on Amazon.com, definitely consider submitting your book for the "Search Inside" program. Buyers appreciate any opportunity to "test drive" a book. Think of the buyers who peruse bookstores for hours picking up and putting back down every book their curious hands touch first. The "Search Inside" feature on Amazon .com does that for online book buyers: It allows them to get a good sense of a book before buying it. Here's a simple breakdown of the instructions:

1. Make sure you work with your publisher or book designer to **get a PDF version of your book**.
2. Go to Amazon.com and **fill out their electronic Participation Agreement Form**.
3. **Wait for an e-mail confirming acceptance** (this takes two to three days) and providing submission instructions.
4. **Submit your PDF directly to Amazon** using provided instructions (it will appear one to two weeks from the upload date).

If you have questions about guidelines or the program, go to the **Search Inside the Book Participation and Submission Guidelines Page**.

can't avoid social media. Though it might feel intense to track the barrage of social media websites that seem to pop up daily, the opportunities for authors are well worth the effort. As an author, you're a content creator as it is. The exchange of ideas, thoughts, and information from content creators is why social media continues to thrive. Social media is a free and effective way to speak directly to your audience and prove that you're offering a valuable product. Like many businesses, you'll discover social media as a way to create new business, follow trends, and establish loyalty with readers. In fact, you could start building a community of followers and readers as soon as you enter the publishing process.

The three primary social media sites to join are Facebook, Twitter, and LinkedIn, which, when used purposefully, will lead to sales. The most rewarding aspect of these sites is the accumulation of "friends" who genuinely become interested in what you have to say. I regularly post links to my favorite articles on self-publishing, writing, and book marketing. I also "follow" the profiles of individuals I respect in the writing and publishing world.

> **The three primary social media sites to join are Facebook, Twitter, and LinkedIn, which, when used purposefully, will lead to sales.**

When I see an update from someone I follow that catches my attention, I share it with others and comment on it. Connecting, interacting, sharing, and occasionally promoting are the ingredients for getting the most out of social media. Avoid overtly marketing your book on social networks, because being sales-y will turn off customers seeking authenticity, and you'll be just another commercial. The rule of thumb in social media marketing is to demonstrate that you are a thought leader. The moment you come across as someone with an agenda, you've lost ground and credibility. This is especially true for Facebook, where your "friends" will block, hide, or "unsubscribe" you the moment you get on their nerves.

Facebook is a savvy tool for authors, because it allows you to create both a profile page as an author and a "fan" page for your book. Do both. Author Gregg Proteaux shared, "I often use Facebook [to promote] my book *Attitudes at Every Altitude,* because it is airline related, and there are several travel- and airline-related groups on Facebook." Posting regular updates on your achievements, sharing your favorite links, and starting conversations are all ways to authentically engage your audience. I like to see authors post photos of book events, ask provocative questions, or post videos of TV appearances. Even further, once on Facebook, you have the ability to "like" the pages of important contacts in the book publishing industry and receive regular updates with vital insider information. Book awards, review publications, other successful authors, independent bookstores, and all the central organizations for publishing have Facebook fan pages. Also, if a moment occurs where you share anything in common with someone of interest, "tag" them in your post, ensuring that not only your followers see it, but that they see it also.

The secrets to conquering Facebook are:

1. To be patient, knowing that it might take several months to achieve measurable results.
2. Post fresh updates frequently. The more fans talk, the better.
3. Don't give them TOO much to talk about. Keep it appropriate to your crowd.

Facebook is also a celebrated forum to run an occasional promotion. Steer clear of coming across as pushy with updates that scream "Buy my book!" However, there are several creative ways to master this art with panache. Offer the fiftieth person to like your book's fan page a free book—which increases your page followers and promotes your book. Offer a 10 percent discount to your Facebook followers in honor of a special month like November, which is National Novel Writing Month, or June, which is National Young Writer's Month. Whenever you meet a new person, mention your Facebook page, and if someone connects with you on Facebook, make sure you acknowledge the connection.

LinkedIn, like Facebook, allows you to create a profile; however, the networks on LinkedIn are professionally oriented. It's a little different than Facebook in that you'll connect first and foremost with other thought leaders and business contacts. Profile

> **LinkedIn is less casual, so your interactions, updates, and connections should be strategic, thoughtful, and mission-driven.**

pictures are important on LinkedIn, so make sure yours is professional. LinkedIn is less casual, so your interactions, updates, and connections should be strategic, thoughtful, and mission-driven. (It's also less addicting than Facebook, so the immediate responses will be fewer.)

Because LinkedIn is a leading site for researching someone, it's positioned to help its users shine creatively. For instance, a LinkedIn profile includes a professional summary that details a person's current projects, special talents, and desired opportunities. There's also the ability to have other LinkedIn users provide recommendations. As an author, you're able to receive recommendations for your book, presentations, blog, or any endeavor enjoyed by others. I've witnessed authors and friends secure speaking opportunities and job interviews and make meaningful connections on LinkedIn. Unlike other social media outlets, daily maintenance isn't as necessary. Devote ample time to creating an impressive profile and from there, visit weekly or even bi-weekly. I make a point to go on LinkedIn once a week, while I make a point to visit Facebook and Twitter daily.

Of the social media trinity, I joined Twitter last and only at the urging of my pals who insisted I was missing out. They were right. Twitter is an online instant messaging system for groups and friends. It's reshaping marketing across the board and impacting the popularity of products worldwide. To give you an idea, Twitter users include 75 percent of the NBA's players, 50 percent of the NFL, 82 percent of the U.S. House, 85 percent of the U.S. Senate, 87 percent of the Billboard Top 100 Musicians, and 93 percent of the top Food Network chefs.[20] I hope you're next if you haven't jumped onboard already. Twitterers or Tweeters (users of Twitter) send short text messages, or tweets, of up to 140 characters that others follow and occasionally respond to.

With a meager 100 million users at press time, Twitter is signing on new users at a rate of two thousand accounts per day. These stats show that such social networking is where it's at. Some have even pegged it "the new TV." Twitter is extremely easy to use from a smartphone, and most users contribute tweets from mobile devices. Here's the deal: If you're as reluctant about Twitter as I admittedly was, take it slow. Start by following people who interest you to get a feel for how it all works. You'll catch on quick if you stick with it. Twitter newbies often panic about attracting followers. An easy approach to gain followers is simply to start following others. Folks on Twitter frequently monitor who follows them and graciously return the favor. Unless you're relatively well known nationally, it takes time and steady tweeting to gain followers in large numbers. Another tip is to retweet updates that spark your interest—retweeting is appreciated and prompts Twitterers to do the same for you. Remember that Twitter is neat because people are choosing to track your activity—it's an opt-in platform. Offer your followers value and the word will spread. Twitter is excellent for word-of-mouth recommendations and buzz building—that grassroots marketing so integral to an indie author's strategy.

Here's a basic game plan for using Facebook, LinkedIn, and Twitter to your advantage:

- **Collect Information**: Follow the Facebook, Twitter, and LinkedIn profiles of *Publisher's Weekly, Writer's Digest, Reader's Digest, Book Business,* and profiles related to your industry. Gather insider information about sales, tips, facts, and recommendations on how to continually engage your audience.
- **Interact:** After you set up your profile on Facebook, Twitter, and LinkedIn, the followers come. Followers will include readers, other authors, contacts, or leads to other contacts. Participate in discussions, ask questions, and share your insight.
- **Find your readers:** Use the "Find People" tool on Twitter, Facebook, and LinkedIn to determine who you want to "follow" as a friend. Search by keyword to generate a list of individuals potentially interested in reading

your book. Use this method to follow and befriend other authors and industry insiders.

- **Generate buzz:** Viral marketing is the ultimate benefit of using Twitter, Facebook, and LinkedIn. Post updates regularly that are related to your book (e.g., book signings, TV appearances, and awards). Followers increase with the number of updates you post.

- **Start Conversations:** The trick to getting the most from using social media is to engage as many people as possible. Ask thought-provoking questions, share your opinions, post links of interest with your reactions to them, and respond to others also starting conversations.

 ## Secrets from Social Media Strategist Tai Goodwin

Technology can seem a little scary—there's always something new and changing. When there are so many other things competing for your time (like finishing your book), social networking might seem like one more thing to add to your already full plate. Here are a few ways to optimize your time and effort when it comes to using networking platforms like Facebook, Twitter, and LinkedIn:

- **Always start with a plan:** You want a roadmap that outlines four things: 1) why you're using social media, 2) what targets or goals you want to reach, 3) how you'll reach those goals, and 4) how you'll track your progress. Having a plan will help you go beyond just "doing" social media to getting results.

- **Find relevant and valuable content to share with your networks:** Use RSS (Really Simple Syndication) feeds to collect posts from your favorite blogs. How it works: RSS readers allow you to collect articles and posts from several sites and have them imported into one screen. Think of it as having a custom magazine rack online. Top tools: Reeder (Mac) or Google Reader.

- **Manage, track, and filter your social media conversations:** Use a dashboard to manage your engagement. Dashboards allow you to view and post to Facebook, Twitter, and LinkedIn from one screen. These dashboards even allow you to schedule your posts in advance. HootSuite (www.hootsuite.com) and Tweet Deck (www.tweetdeck.com) are the top two dashboards.

- **Find people to follow using LinkedIn Groups and Twellow:** Twellow (www.twellow.com) is the Yellow Pages for Twitter. And most LinkedIn groups will have a discussion where members add their Facebook pages. Between those two options you'll find meaningful and relevant connections. Make sure you add your own profile to Twellow and add a link to your Facebook page on LinkedIn so people can find and follow you too.

- **Create a YouTube video:** Just like movies have trailers that capture an audience's attention, you can create one for your book using YouTube. Keep in mind that your YouTube video can take many formats. For instance, your video could show you sitting at a desk or at a different location, or it could be an animated PowerPoint slideshow converted to video. Some of the most shared videos are just powerful images and quotes set to music. Try a tool like Animoto (www.animoto.com) to create a trailer highlighting your book and then post it to YouTube.

Goodwin shared that most people with a successful business initially start slow with social media. "Getting started with social networking may not feel easy, but that doesn't mean it has to be overwhelming," explained Goodwin.

Contact Tai Goodwin at tai@taigoodwin.com.

The Benefits of Author Blogging

I'm the first to admit, it's not easy to blog every week. But blogging is a simple and free tool that could easily become the most effective strategy in your inventory. Even if you don't decide to become a blogger, target bloggers as an instrument in helping promote and market your book. The trick to effective blogging is to become a valuable resource. An author's blog can be about his book, or even about the journey of writing and publishing a book. Go with the direction that doesn't feel like a chore. If a blog goes more than a week without an update, followers lose attention, so choose the track that excites you the most. Authors ask me regularly what they should post on their blogs, and frankly, whether it's worth it to blog. I believe that authors should try their hand at creating a blog because it creates such a remarkable opportunity to connect with readers, discover new readers, and (let's not forget) keep you writing.

Bloggers have become celebrities in their own right, and in many ways are more instrumental in discovering new talent than newspaper and magazine reporters. Many bloggers are also indie authors, making them ideal candidates to enlist for supporting your book. I suggest that you target bloggers for book reviews, send press releases to well-known bloggers on your book's topic, and track bloggers with a strong presence (i.e., followers, fans, and traffic) on Facebook and Twitter. Some blogs are as well visited as news and large corporate websites. Bloggers are often invited to guest blog on other blogs, which is a tried-and-true strategy for an indie author trying to expand his or her reach. Bloggers are also often willing to allow someone to guest blog on their sites. Ken Thurber, author of *Big Wave Surfing: Extreme Technology Development, Management, Marketing & Investing,* shared,

> *In marketing my book, I struck several deals with small business blogs for content outlets to keep the book in the public eye as sales began. Today these deals are still in place. I also write blogs for a number of bloggers who resell the book.*

If you decide to venture into the blogosphere, here's my checklist of helpful blog ideas to keep the content flowing:

- **The ten key points of your platform:** Regularly refresh lists that tie-in to your book's major selling points, including quick how-to's and anecdotes.

- **Photos related to your book:** Make sure you post photos of book events, award ceremonies, conferences, and workshops.

- **News related to your topic:** If there's news related to your topic or platform, post it, even if it's only a link to a news article. Your blog readers will appreciate your keeping them informed. Make sure the source is legit and current.

- **News about you:** Whenever you're in the news, post a link to the video, article, radio interview, or guest blog. Also, keep your blog readers informed about awards your book wins. Remember that even as a finalist for an award, you're considered an award winner!

- **Review a resource:** When your content supply is running low, review a product, service, or resource important to your audience. Maybe it's a book you read that you think your audience would love. Be careful not to come across like you're "plugging" something for somebody else; however, giving sincere reasons why you like or didn't like something is always appreciated.

- **What you're up to:** Keep your blog followers updated on what you're doing. Are you working on another book? Did you just meet *your* favorite author? Planning a book tour? Tell your readers; they'll follow for as long as you engage them.

- **Post an answer to a question you've been asked:**
  This is a quick way to engage your followers and demon-strate your expertise—both are good things!

 ## Ease on Down the Aisle—the App Store Aisle!

If you have an Android phone, iPhone, iPad, or iPod, take the time to peruse the Android or iTunes app store for the latest and greatest writing-related apps. I'll assume you have the basic must-have apps: Google, Nook or Kindle, and Wikipedia. Here are more of my favorites to jumpstart your app shopping; most are free, and none are more than $2.00.

WordPress

WordPress has quickly become the most preferred platform for bloggers. The WordPress phone app is complete with the ability to upload your blog post, highlight the location from where you've uploaded it, and insert high-resolution photos. If you think blogging is not for you, the ability to do everything from your mobile phone might change your mind.

Merriam-Webster Dictionary

The classic resource every writer needs at his fingertips is even more accessible—and free. The Merriam-Webster app provides all the value of a dictionary plus voice search if you don't know the spelling of a word. It also has an integrated thesaurus, audio pronunciation, and word of the day tool, and tracks your recent history. If there was ever an app with the works, this is it.

B-Rhymes

A neat app for poets, children's books authors, and wordsmiths, this rhyming dictionary app generates a comprehensive list of rhyming words and also "words that sound good together even though they don't technically rhyme." It boasts a catalog of more than 40,000 words and allows you to save your favorites.

Idea Organizer

Like a personal stash of sticky notes on your phone or tablet, this app allows you to store and organize your writing ideas. What makes this app neat is not only the ability to type your thought in text form, but also the ability to voice record your idea or use your phone's camera to take visual notes. With Idea Organizer you can e-mail notes to your computer and also share notes with friends.

iTalk Recorder Premium

If you like to record your thoughts before putting them on paper, this app is for you. iTalk is one of the leading full-featured recording apps that allow you to append, organize, and share recordings. It also provides multiple levels of recording quality and easy transfer to e-mail. An app like this would be handy for interviews, book meetings, and recording presentations.

- Remember that the Internet gives readers more power than ever before to explore the books that are out there. Use this to your advantage and create a presence so they find you easily.
- Only engage in the Internet options that you like and will enjoy long term. If you can't blog regularly or don't enjoy doing it, it's probably not for you. But perhaps you'll have fun doing a monthly newsletter instead.
- Even if you're not participating in the Internet trends of the moment, you should still be informed about how they work and what they are. Keeping yourself in the know will empower your book's long-term relevance.

Indie Author Wisdom

"Once my book went to the printer, I began aggressively marketing it using a combination of three key Internet tools: my website, Facebook, and Twitter. Well before the book was available, I launched www.bigwavesurfing.com. My website's homepage has strong selling points for the book and offers an online newsletter that users can sign up for. The newsletter generates a list of important contacts and additional sales leads."

~Ken Thurber, author of *Big Wave Surfing: Extreme Technology Development, Management, Marketing & Investment*

The Final Word

You Are Your Own Gatekeeper

Indie authors include current best-selling authors E. Lynn Harris, Vince Flynn, E.L. James, William P. Young, and countless others who refused to let the publishing industry determine the destiny of their books. Much has been said about self-publishing. Over the years, it has taken a beating—and, some would argue, rightfully so. Questions about quality swirl at the center of the self-publishing debate.

The truth is this: The revolution has come. Good authors with good books—and the sales to prove it—have brought self-publishing out of the "dark." Like indie filmmakers and indie musicians, the indie author community is more multidimensional than publishing insiders ever thought it could be. Even the big publishing powerhouses have started to change their point of view. And soon, they'll be trying to imitate us.

Authors now have options outside the usual route of finding an agent and hoping for that big book deal. They are pushing and expanding this industry, and they, not publishers, are now the gatekeepers. As the publishing industry evolves, we'll continue to see self-published books take center stage. As it is, the industry has turned on its heels.

How has self-publishing come such a long way? It's simple: because of authors like you. Today's indie authors are not like the authors of yesterday, with long-shot hopes of writing a best seller and becoming a household name. Okay—while we all secretly (or not so secretly) want to sell millions of copies, indie authors are motivated by forces other than profit—and it is this difference that readers have come to notice and respect.

Authors are writing books to accompany well-attended seminars and workshops they've developed. They're writing books to comple-ment and grow successful companies they've started. They're writing books to improve their communities. They're writing books to share their war stories, their sacred rituals, their memories, their philoso-phies, and their visions. They're writing books and they're doing it without waiting for permission. These authors have used self-publish-ing to accomplish their goals and live their dreams. While many large royalty-based publishing houses are driven by profit, indie authors must be inspired by purpose. They have officially upped the ante. They're passionate, they're winning prestigious awards, they're getting paid for their work, and they're not losing momentum anytime soon.

What does that mean for you? If you have an idea and the enthu-siasm to bring it to fruition, go for it. Just the other day, an author, (let's call her Sarah) sat across from me discussing her plans to pub-lish a coaching book for parents. She said, "I can't believe I'm actually going to do this. But it makes sense." I could see the wheels turning as Sarah started to list the ways she'd use her book and how it would help people. Sarah is a counselor, and families consistently rely on her for advice. Her practice is starting to gain traction. She explained, "People have asked me to write a book, and I always thought, 'Really? I should?' Now, I believe my book would perfectly complement all that I'm meant to do."

I've worked with authors like Sarah for years, and I guarantee she'll create a successful book that enlightens, empowers, and engages her readers all while doing what she loves—helping parents and families.

You know what your purpose is, or you wouldn't be reading this book. You wouldn't be reading all the way to the last page, and the wheels wouldn't be turning in your head, and you wouldn't be imagining someone reading the last page of your book. Yes, *your* book. I want you to get your book written. Get it done, get it out there, and then send it to me, because I want to see it. I want to read your book. And then together, we'll carry on the Indie Author Revolution.

Bibliography

Auletta, Ken. "Publish or Perish: Can the iPad Topple the Kindle, and Save the Book Business?" *The New Yorker*, April 26, 2010.

Chick, BScheife. "How a Self-Published Author Scored a Big New York Publisher." *ForeWord Magazine*, January 2010: 64.

Fowler, A. Geoffrey, and A. Marie Baca. "The ABCs of E-Reading." *The Wall Street Journal*, August 25, 2010: D1–D2.

Greco, Albert N. *The Book Publishing Industry.* Mahwah: Lawrence Erlbaum Associates, Inc., Publishers, 2005.

Kasdorf, William E. *The Columbia Guide to Digital Publishing.* New York: Columbia University Press, 2003.

Katz, Christina. *Get Known Before the Book Deal: Use Your Personal Strengths to Grow an Author Platform.* Cincinnati: Writer's Digest Books, 2008.

Survey, Book Industry Study Group.

Trachtenberg, Jefferey A. "Authors Feel Pinch in Age of E-books." *The Wall Street Journal*, September 28, 2010: A1, A18.

Appendix A:
Glossary of Terms

Advanced Reader Copy (ARCs): see Galley

Agent: An individual representing an author in his or her negotiations with a publisher. Agents might also handle or offer other services, like copyright matters. They receive a percentage of royalties paid to the author.

Amazon.com: Internet-based book retailer started in 1995, which also sells other merchandise, including e-books. They are also the creator of the Kindle e-reader and CreateSpace, an online self-publishing company.

BN.com: Barnes & Noble's book-selling website.

Back Matter: The pages located at the back of the book, i.e. order forms, notes pages, author biography, permissions, credits, glossary, and resources.

Barcode: An optical machine-readable representation of data, which shows certain information on certain products. On a book, the ISBN and sometimes the price are represented with a barcode on the back cover.

Barnes & Noble: One of the largest book retailers or bookstore chains in the United States, also the creator of the Nook e-reader.

Bind: To fasten printed sheets or signatures with wire, thread, glue, or by other means.

Bleed: Printing that extends to the edge of a sheet or page after trimming.

Blurb: A favorable quote(s) used on the front or back cover of the book, usually provided by someone prominent or well known whose opinion adds credibility to the book. Also referred to as a testimonial or endorsement.

Book Design: The process of organizing and developing the final printer-ready version of a book, factoring its physical and visual aesthetic (i.e., its cover, trim size, and graphics).

Book Designer: An individual who executes the design of a book, including its cover and interior design. Also referred to as a graphic designer or graphic artist.

Book Signing: A planned event in which the author signs copies of his/her book. Usually takes place at a bookstore, conferences, trade shows, and speaking engagements.

C1S: Abbreviation for "coated on one side," used to describe cover or text paper that is coated on one side only.

C2S: Abbreviation for "coated on two sides," used to describe cover or text paper that is coated on both sides.

Case: The covers enclosing a book, usually made of thick cardboard and normally covered with cloth, paper, or leather.

Case Bind: To bind using glue to hold signatures to a case made of binder board covered with fabric, plastic, or leather. Also called cloth bind, edition bind, hard bind, or hard cover.

CIP: A Cataloging in Publication record (CIP data) is a bibliographic record prepared by the Library of Congress for a book that has not yet been published. When the book is published, the publisher includes the CIP data on the copyright page, thereby facilitating book processing for libraries and book dealers.

Coated Paper: Clay-coated printing paper with a smooth finish.

Copy: All furnished material or disk used in the production of a printed product.

Copyright: A bundle of exclusive rights to permit or forbid the use of a work. In the United States, copyright is granted to the author of the work, the author's employer, or anyone to whom rights are legally transferred.

Copyright Page: The page that normally appears on the verso of the title page, containing the artistic property protection along with publisher information, CIP data, and ISBN.

Digital Color Printing: The use of multiple print heads that place specified colors of inks in predetermined places. The results are similar to photographs, but are often larger. This printing method is used in smaller print runs of 500 books or less.

DPI (dots per inch): A measurement of resolution for a printer or scanner. For example, a resolution of 300 dpi means 300 dots across and 300 dots down. A higher dpi signals a higher or finer resolution.

Dust Jacket: A separate and removable paper covering for a case-bound or hardcover book. It often includes promotional copy.

E-book: An electronic copy of a book viewed through various mediums, including on the computer screen as a PDF file or on an e-book reader.

E-book Reader: A device created for reading book content (e.g., Nook, Sony E-Reader, Kobo, Kindle, and iPad).

Editor: A person who reviews and provides suggestions for improving upon a manuscript, often referred to as a copy editor, line editor, or manuscript editor.

Editing: The process of making corrections to a manuscript, factoring consistency, clarity, and focus.

Emboss: Pressing an image into paper so that it will create a raised treatment.

End Sheet: Sheet that attaches the inside papers of a case-bound book to its cover. Also called end papers.

Estimate: Price that states what a publishing service will probably cost. These costs are based on specifications provided by the author and/or publisher. Also called a bid or quote.

Flap Copy: Book summary text that is placed on the inside portion of a book cover.

Front Matter: The pages preceding the text of a book, i.e., title, copyright, dedication, foreword, and table of contents. Usually unnumbered or numbered with roman numerals.

Galley: A bound manuscript created after typesetting used for pre-publication marketing. Also referred to as advance reader copy (ARCs) or book review copy.

Genre: The classification of a book's subject, such as business, biography, poetry, and fiction. The genre is usually indicated on the back cover of a book.

Hard Copy: The output of a computer printer, or printed pages of a manuscript.

Hard Proof: A printed proof supplied by the printer distinguished from a *soft proof*, which is an electronic proof viewed on a computer screen.

Header: Information, such as page number or chapter title, that appears at the top of every page of a book.

Insert: A printed piece prepared for insertion into a book during the printing phase, usually photographs, maps, etc.

ISBN (International Standard Book Number): A thirteen-digit number specific to publishers that uniquely identifies books for purchasing and inventory purposes. Individual authors can purchase an ISBN from myidentifiers.com.

Laminate: A thin, transparent plastic sheet (coating) applied to a thick stock (covers, postcards, etc.) providing protection against liquids and heavy use, and usually accenting existing color, providing a glossy (or lens) effect.

Landscape: A book orientation in which the finished book is wider than it is tall and binds on the short side. Also referred to as oblong.

Lay-Flat Bind: Method of perfect binding that allows a publication to lie fully open. Also known as lay-flat perfect binding.

Matte Finish: Dull paper, laminate, or ink finish.

Mentoring Press: A hybrid publisher that guides authors with marketable manuscripts through the self-publishing process. Mentoring presses offer services for a fee that include coaching, editing, book design, printing, publicity and distribution. Mentoring presses are often selective and emphasize the importance of editing and good design to create successful books.

Mission Statement: A brief description of a company's (or book's) purpose and what it hopes to accomplish.

Native Files: The original files from which a designer creates a books within a desktop publishing software program like Adobe InDesign.

Offset Paper: Term for uncoated book paper.

Offset Printing: Printing technique that transfers ink from a plate to a blanket to paper rather than directly from plate to paper.

Over-Runs or Overs: Copies printed in excess of the specified quantity. (Printing trade terms allow for plus or minus 10 percent to represent complete order.)

Page Count: Total number of pages that a publication has, including blank pages.

Page Proof: Proof of type and graphics as they will look on the finished page, complete with elements such as headings, rules, and folios.

Pagination: The numbering of pages, or the order in which pages appear in a book.

Perfect Bind: To bind sheets that have been ground at the spine and are held to the cover by glue. Also called adhesive bind, cutback bind, glue bind, paper bind, patent bind, perfecting bind, soft bind, or soft cover.

Plate: Piece of paper, metal, plastic, or rubber carrying an image to be reproduced using a printing press.

Platform: An author's existing following, media presence, or outlet to promote and market his or her book.

PMS: The abbreviated name of the Pantone Color Matching System®.

POD (Print-On-Demand): A digital printing technology suitable for small runs (twenty to five hundred book copies) printed and bound in much less time than traditional printing and binding methods.

Point: For paper, a unit of thickness equaling 1/1000 inch.

Prepress: The process of setup and preparing artwork, film, and screens for conventional printing methods.

Press Check: Event at which makeready sheets from the press are examined before authorizing the start of full production.

Press Time: Amount of time that it takes for a book to be printed, including time required for setup.

Proofread: To examine a manuscript for errors such as misspellings, typos, incorrect grammar, and incorrect usage of punctuation. This is separate from the copyediting stage and takes place after a book has been formatted by a book designer.

Public Relations (PR): A form of marketing that engages consumers through media coverage, events, and social media.

Publicity: An aspect of public relations that focuses on the media to generate sales leads and create sales demand.

Reprint: A second or additional printing after a first or initial print run. Often needed after all books from a first printing have been consumed.

Request for Quote (RFQ): A proposal created by the author or publisher to acquire quotes for publishing services such as design or printing.

Return: An unsold book returned to the bookseller or distributor for a full refund within a specified time period, usually six months.

Royalty: The author's portion or percentage of book's net sales income. An author might have a negotiated royalty in a contract with a publisher.

Serif Font: A typeface that has curved edges on each letter, making it easier to read. An example of a serif font would be Times New Roman. The opposite of a serif font is *sans serif* and an example would be Arial.

Special Sales: Unusual or nontraditional outlets for selling books (e.g., organizations, government institutions, and book clubs), usually in mass or bulk quantities.

Spine: The binding edge or backbone of a book or publication where the title is displayed when it is standing upright on a shelf.

Spot Varnish: Varnish used to highlight a specific part of a printed sheet.

Spread: Two facing pages in a book.

Title: The name of a book. (Note: Titles are not able to be copyrighted under the law.)

Title Page: A page in the front matter of a book that lists the book's title.

Trim Size: The size of the printed material in its finished stage (e.g., the finished trim size is 5.5" x 8.5").

Typesetting: The process of transforming a manuscript into a form suitable for printing. Includes the selection of typefaces, type size, chapter and header treatments, and performing page-layout in a program such as Adobe InDesign.

Uncoated Paper: Paper that has not been coated with clay. Also called offset paper.

Vanity Press: A company that helps authors self-publish, offering book design and printing services for a fee regardless of quality and marketability.

Appendix B:
Resource Directory

My Favorite Books on Writing

- *Merriam-Webster's Manual for Writers & Editors: A Clear, Authoritative Guide to Effective Writing and Publishing,* Editors of Merriam-Webster's Collegiate Dictionary
- *The Portable MFA in Creative Writing,* The New York Writers Workshop
- *The Only Writing Book You'll Ever Need: A Complete Resource for Perfecting Any Type of Writing,* Pamela Rice Hahn

My Favorite Books on Publishing

- *Self-Publishing Manual: How to Write, Print, and Sell Your Own Book,* Dan Poynter
- *Self-Publishing 101,* Debbie Elicksen

- *The Well-Fed Self-Publisher: How to Turn One Book Into a Full-Time Living*, Peter Bowerman
- *Publishing for Profit: Successful Bottom-Line Management for Book Publishers*, Thomas Woll
- *The Book Publishing Industry*, Albert N. Greco

My Favorite Books on Marketing

- *The Author's Guide to Building an Online Platform*, Stephanie Chandler
- *Publicize Your Book: An Insider's Guide to Getting Your Book the Attention It Deserves*, Jacqueline Deval
- *Grassroots Marketing for Authors and Publishers*, Shel Horowitz
- *Get Known Before the Book Deal: Use Your Personal Strengths to Grow an Author Platform*, Christina Katz
- *The New Rules of Marketing & PR: How to Use News Releases, Blogs, Podcasting, Viral Marketing & Online Media to Reach Buyers Directly*, David Meerman Scott
- *1001 Ways to Market Your Book for Authors and Publishers*, John Kremer
- *Red Hot Internet Publicity*, Penny C. Sansevieri
- *Jump Start Your Book Sales: A Money-Making Guide for Authors, Independent Publishers and Small Presses*, Marilyn & Tom Ross

Recommended Blogs

- There Are No Rules Blog: blog.writersdigest.com/norules
- Book Marketing Bestsellers Book Promotion Blog: blog.bookmarket.com

- Publishing Trends Blog: www.publishingtrends.com
- The Self-Publishing Insider: theselfpublishingblog.com
- The Book Designer: www.thebookdesigner.com
- A Newbie's Guide to Publishing: www.jakonrath.blogspot.com
- Duolit: www.theselfpublishingteam.com
- Christina Katz's Blog: www.kristinakatz.com
- Jane Friedman's Blog: www.janefriedman.com
- The Creative Penn: www.thecreativepenn.com
- Wise, Ink: www.wiseinkblog.com
- Editorial Inspirations: www.editorialinspirations.com

Book Review Sources

- Midwest Book Review, www.midwestbookreview.com
- Foreword Magazine, www.forewordmagazine.com
- Reader Views, www.readerviews.com
- GalleyCat, www.mediabistro.com/galleycat
- Indie Reader, www.indiereader.com

Book Award Resources

- Moonbeam Book Awards (Children's Books): www.moonbeam awards.com
- Ben Franklin Awards: www.ibpa–online.org/pubresources/ benfrank.aspx
- Book of the Year Awards: www.bookoftheyearawards.com
- Writer's Digest International Self-Published Book Awards: www.writersdigest.com/selfpublished

- Independent Book Publisher Award (IPPY): www.independent-publisher.com/ipland/IPAwards.php
- National Indie Excellence Awards: www.indieexcellence.com

Online Resources

- **Authorlink for Editors, Agents, Writers, and Readers**. Provides publishing news, information, and marketing services for editors, agents, producers, writers, and readers. www.authorlink.com
- **Bookwire**. Powered by Bowker's Books In Print® database, this site is the ultimate book search engine and also provides helpful resources and links. www.bookwire.com
- **Literary Market Place**. The directory of more than 30,000 American and Canadian companies, literary agencies, books, periodicals, awards, courses, and events in the publishing world. A vital resource for anyone looking for publishing industry data. www.literarymarketplace.com
- **Para Publishing**. Dan Poynter, a celebrated guru in the self-publishing world, has a website that provides lots of excellent information, free documents, and statistics. www.parapublishing.com
- **Independent Book Publishers Association**. The IBPA is the largest not-for-profit trade association representing independent book publishers, which also includes indie authors. Their publication *Independent* is chock-full of insightful articles, book publishing resources, and marketing opportunities for small indie publishers and authors. www.ibpa-online.org
- **SPANnet**. The Small Publishers Association of North America (SPAN) is an active, enthusiastic community of authors and pub-

lishers providing writing, marketing, book production, and other resources. The website is open to anyone and offers useful information on trends, news, and upcoming publishing events. www.spannet.org

- **The Authors Guild.** The Authors Guild has been the nation's leading advocate for writers' interests in effective copyright protection, fair contracts, and free expression since 1912. It provides legal assistance and a broad range of web services to its members. www.authorsguild.org

- **Publishers Lunch.** Publishers Lunch is regarded as one of the industry's "daily essential reads." Each report gathers the latest stories from all over the web and print about the publishing industry. www.lunch.publishersmarketplace.com

- **The Chicago Manual of Style Website.** A well-traveled website for editors, writers, and students. Provides style guide tools and a useful Q&A, and offers the subscription-only electronic version of the *Chicago Manual of Style.* www.chicagomanualofstyle.org

- **Publisher's Weekly.** The *Publisher's Weekly* publication and website are the best resources for following the publishing industry. Though slanted more toward royalty publishing, PW is quickly recognizing the indie author and self-publishing movement and even offers a review service for self-published books. www.publishersweekly.com

- **Writer's Digest.** The most distinguished writer-centric website, which includes the best online database for journal submissions around, providing invaluable news, marketing, and writers' conferences links. www.writersdigest.com

Booksellers and Bookshops Resources

- **Amazon.com Advantage**. Advantage is a self-service consignment program that promotes and sells media products directly on Amazon.com. Advantage is designed specifically for publishers and authors. www.amazon.com
- **American Booksellers Association**. The nonprofit organization representing independent bookstores nationwide. www.bookweb.org
- **Baker & Taylor**. Supplier of books, movies, music, and information products to libraries and retailers worldwide. www.btol.com
- **Indiebound**. National online portal for locating independent bookstores. Indiebound.org
- **BookWeb**. The homepage of the American Booksellers Association. www.bookweb.com
- **Ingram Book Group**. One of the largest wholesalers of books, movies, music, and information to libraries and retailers nationwide. www.ingrambookgroup.com

Copyrights, ISBN, Standards, and Legal Resources

- **Book Industry Study Group**: www.bisg.org
- **Bowker.com**: Source for book, serial, and publishing data.
- **ISBN.org**: Everything about International Standard Book Numbers (ISBN) and Standard Address Numbers (SAN).
- **Intellectual Property and Technology Law**, www.irwl.com: Providing legal services in copyrights, trademarks, and trade secrets; acquiring and publishing content in print, broadcast, and

online media; and electronic commerce-areas of growing opportunity for its clients in the Information Age.

- **Library of Congress**, www.loc.org: The Library of Congress is the nation's oldest federal cultural institution with more than 130 million items on approximately 530 miles of bookshelves.
- **The Publishing Law Center**, www.publaw.com: Legal information for the publishing community.
- **U.S. Copyright Office**: www.loc.gov/copyright
- **Unipat**: Patents, trademarks, copyrights, and licensing, www.unipat.org

Organizations and Associations

- **American Library Association**: www.ala.org
- **Association of Publishers Marketing Association American Publishers**: www.publishers.org
- **Book Industry Study Group**: www.bisg.org
- **Midwest Independent Publishers Association**, www.Mipa .org: Organization in the Midwest comprised of authors, independent publishers, and publishing vendors.
- **The Loft**, www.loft.org: Leading writing center located in Minneapolis, Minnesota, that offers classes, workshops, and conferences for writers of every genre.

Publishing Magazines and Newsletters

- Foreword Magazine: www.forewordmagazine.com
- Independent: www.ibpa-online.org
- Library Journal: www.libraryjournal.com

- Publisher's Weekly: www.pw.org
- PMA Newsletter: www.pma-online.org

My Favorite Author Websites

- Colleen Baldrica: www.colleenbaldrica.com
- Susie Bazil: www.thesickbug.com
- Robin Dedeker: www.momentsofintuition.com
- Brian Duren: www.brianduren.com
- Gordy Fredrickson: www.gordonfredrickson.com
- Sarah Fritz, Paula Johnson, and Thea Zitzow: www.uflipp.com
- Marilyn Jax: www.marilynjax.com
- Patrick Mader: www.patrickmader.com
- Tim Munkeby: www.timmunkeby.com
- Amy Recob: www.thebugabees.com
- Suzanne Ruff: www.thereluctantdonor.com
- DeAnne and Michelle Sherman: www.seedsofhopebooks.com
- Deirdre Van Nest: www.fireyourfear.com
- Derek Wolden: www.basketcasesbook.com

Appendix C:
Samples

After 28 Years, Local Police Officer
Reveals the Behind the Scenes of Law Enforcement

"I was the type who did not share work stories with anyone,
including my family, but I never buried them…"

– Richard Greelis

(June 26, 2014—Minneapolis, MN) Whether encouraging his cowering K-9 to reengage during a crime in progress, or interviewing an unrepentant shoe molester, veteran cop Richard Greelis, author of *COPBOOK* reveals true stories of life, death, and the cops who manage the space between them. Having spent much of his career investigating sex crimes, Greelis gives readers a personal view of law enforcement in his new memoir, *COPBOOK* (Beaver's Pond Press, June 2009). *COPBOOK* is both candid and at other times, painfully tragic.

Greelis, a native of Robbinsdale, MN had no interest in police work as a child. He graduated from the University of MN in 1980 and then worked as a realtor, before finally deciding to enter the Police Skills Program in 1981. It wasn't long before he was hired by the Bloomington Police Department and began his 28-year career in law enforcement.

Greelis draws on his career as a street cop, a SWAT team operator, a detective in both the Violent Crimes and Sex Crimes Units, and an undercover Intel investigator for the 2008 Republican National Convention. Greelis also served as a task force member on the FBI's Joint Terrorism Task Force following the 9/11 attacks. In talking about his experience, Greelis states, "Like every career cop, I've witnessed enough death and misery to last several lifetimes, and have been forced to answer some weighty questions."

As Greelis approaches retirement, he answered those weighty questions and says, "I had the desire to write…to record some of my more memorable experiences while they were still fresh in my mind." Greelis makes clear that his purpose for writing his memoir is to allow insight into the experiences of victims whose stories are seldom told and into the experiences of the officers who attend those victims.

As retirement begins for Greelis this July, of his career in law enforcement he states, "I'm satisfied I chose the right career. Like being cast in a never-ending saga of tragedy, comedy, action, and intrigue, there is really nothing quite like it."

About the Author

Richard Greelis has been in law enforcement 28 years. He lives in Blooming-ton, MN with his beautiful wife and three brilliant sons. He'll launch his book with a party in Bloomington, MN on July 9th, followed by a segment on the *Lori & Julia Show* (FM107) on July 14th at 4:30pm.

Copbook: A Memoir by Richard Greelis

Price: $14.95
Pub Date: June 2009
ISBN: 978-1-59298-282-0
Pages: 413 pages, Softcover, 5.5 x 8.5
To order visit: www.copbook.net or www.bookhousefulfillment.com or call 800-901-3480

For Immediate Release

Transfixing Novel Reveals the Allure of Northern Minnesotan Town

Minneapolis, MN—Minnesotans, some of the bravest and most weather-tolerant people in the world, could never be anything but proud of their unparalleled winters. Maybe it's the mysterious, ominous, yet nostalgic feeling that comes from the first real blizzard—or "whiteout"—of the season that they really look forward to all summer long. To that end, Minnesota native Brian Duren has the perfect summer read for all of those beach loungers longing for the return of the frigid, blustering, and bone-chilling sub-zero temperatures.

Whiteout, Duren's first novel, is based upon a classic Minnesotan "whiteout." American expatriate Paul Bauer, a freelance journalist living in Paris with his French lover, thinks he has it made. Upon his mother's death, he returns to a little town in northern Minnesota for the funeral. There, he encounters unsettling contradictions to his understanding of his family history and begins asking the question—his family has always wanted to prevent him from asking: What really did happen in that whiteout thirty-five years ago?

Mary Logue, author of *Point No Point,* says, "The atmosphere of the north woods permeates the novel and gives it a deep claustrophobic, gothic sense... *Whiteout* is an intense, moving story about how lost a family can get and how it can right itself again." Logue is a winner of the Minnesota Book Award for Fiction.

Brian Duren has taught at the Universities of Texas, Tulsa, Iowa, and Minnesota. He eventually left teaching, became an administrator at the University of Minnesota, and then retired in 2004 to devote more time to writing and to his three sons. Duren has a doctorate in French literature from the University of Paris, a B.A. in English and a Ph.D. in French from the University of Minnesota. *Whiteout* is his first published novel. He is currently in the process of completing his next novel, *Every Tom, Dick, and Harry.*

More information on *Whiteout* can be found **www.brianduren.com**
Contact Brian: brian@BrianDuren.com

SAMPLE MARKETING PLAN OUTLINE

1. Overview

- What is your book about? (1 paragraph)
- Why did you write it?

2. What makes this book unique?

- How is your book different from other books on the market?
- List 3 key messages you want to convey to readers about the value of your book. (This is also described as your platform.)

3. Target Market

- Who will buy your book?
- Why is the subject matter important to your target market?
- List 3 newsworthy story ideas that could be used to intrigue media and buyers to review/buy your book.

4. Competition

- Which books will your book most closely compete with?
- What sets your book apart from your competition?

5. Geographical areas

- Are there geographical areas where you want to sell your book?

6. Promotion Strategy

- General areas
- Results Expected
- Short term
- Long term

7. Promotional Activities Planned (add brief list under each item)

- Review Contacts
- Launch events
- Readings
- Book signing events
- Presentations
- Radio interviews
- TV interviews
- Print interviews
- Exhibits
- Conferences
- Trade shows
- Professional associations
- Other events

Book Title:

101 Ways to Peaceful Living

Genre:

Body, Mind & Spirit, Zen, Meditation

Purpose Statement:

To provide stimulating methods for overcoming stress, fatigue, and depression.

Book Summary:

101 Ways to Peaceful Living is a simple guide to help the busy and overworked individual find calm in their everyday routines. Presented in short and straight-forward tips, readers will collect key tools to cultivate peaceful living, such as:

- Learning breathing exercises to induce restful sleep
- Creating "mini-vacations" without leaving the comfort of home
- Discovering foods scientifically proven to positively affect emotional health

Key Book Strengths:

- Written from the perspective of someone who works with clinically depressed individuals
- Provides exercises and concrete solutions proven to help individuals suffering with emotional health issues
- Success stories from ten individuals

Target Market (Buyer Profiles):

The new parent—new parents, predominantly mothers, who struggle with poor sleeping habits, postpartum depression, and fatigue. Ideal for new parents who routinely seek solace through yoga, acupuncture, and psychotherapy.

Professionals (ages 27 – 55)—business professionals who are overwrought with pressure to work long hours, who forgo vacations and personal time, and who put work before personal well being.

Spiritual Seekers of any age or gender—the spiritually open who are familiar with meditative practices, breathing therapies, and mindful thinking.

Author Biography and credentials:

Nancy Quaker has been a life and wellness coach for more than fifteen years. In 2004, she launched The Peaceful Living Foundation, which helps individuals seeking balance and reduced stress through coaching services, workshops, and online seminars. Nancy appears regularly as a conference speaker and media commentator. She has articles published in *Living Well* magazine. For more information visit, www.nancyquaker.com.

Competing Titles:

* *Living a Peaceful Life* by Dr. Robert Puff
* *Patience: The Art of Peaceful Living* by Allan Lokos
* *Peaceful Living: Daily Meditations for Living with Love, Healing, and Compassion* by Mary Mackenzie
* *The Quiet Mind: Imagery For Peaceful Living* by Gerald Jampolsky and Diane Cirincione

Marketing Strategy:

* Partnership with the Health Resource Network, which founded National Stress Awareness Day (April 16)
* Launching a "Just Say No To Stress" campaign, which will aim to have 25,000 individuals pledge to reduce their stress by January 1, 2015
* Launching a direct mail campaign to drive bookstore sales
* Appearances at bookstores, yoga centers, health and wellness centers, and at conferences related to health, fitness, nutrition, and spirituality
* Online marketing includes website, blogging, e-newsletter, Facebook fan page, and Twitter account
* Targeting health publications, news stations, and websites

Financials

Publishing Services Checklist/Costs:

Service	Vendor Name	Estimated Cost
Project Management	The Book Genies	$1,000
Ghostwriting	n/a	n/a
Editing	M. Brian	$1,200
Book Design	The Book Genies Designer	$2,000
Proofreading	The Book Genies Proofreader	$500
Galley Printing	n/a	n/a
Book Printing	The Book Genies Printer	$4,000
E-Book Services	The Book Genies E-Book Service	$400
Website Services	Author Websites R Us	$800
Marketing:		
Event Planning	Myself	$200
Media Kit	Myself	$25
Social Media Services	Myself	n/a
Publicity Services	Rocky Star, Publicist	$500
Distribution	Book Genies Distribution Service	$50 per month
Illustration	n/a	n/a
Miscellaneous:		
Miscellaneous:		

Publishing Timeline:

Service	Start-Date	Projected Deadline
Project Management	Ongoing	Ongoing
Ghostwriting	n/a	n/a
Editing	March 1	April 15
Book Design	April 20	May 30
Proofreading	May 15	May 21
Galley Printing	n/a	n/a
Website Services	May 15	June 15
E-Book Services	May 30	June 30
Book Printing	May 30	July 5

SAMPLE COPYRIGHT PAGE

ISBN: 978-1-XXXXX-XXX-X
Library of Congress Number: 2015XXXXXX

Printed in the United States of America
First Printing: 2015

19   18   17   16   15   5   4   3   2   1

Cover and Interior Design by:

Anyone Publishing, Inc.
2234 Main Street, Suite 112
Anycity, State 55432
www.anyonepublishing.com

To order visit www.anyonepublishing.com
Or call (800) 555-5555. Reseller Discounts available.

Appendix D:
Copyrighting Your Material

Copyrighting Your Material

For the record, according to the copyright act of 1976, as soon as your work is created, by law, you own the copyright as the author. Thus, it is not a legal requirement to register your work with the Register of Copyrights at the Library of Congress. However, if you'd like to take the added step of protecting your work, do so. Registering your work, by the way, does establish its "birth" date in the event you ever have to deal with copyright infringement. There are two requirements for copyrighting work:

1. It has to be an author's original work.
2. It has to be in a tangible medium of expression (i.e., it must be on paper, video, CD, or an uploadable file).

There are also several categories of material that are not copyrightable. These include:

- Works not in a fixed or tangible form
- Titles, names, short phrases, and slogans
- Listings of ingredients or contents
- Ideas, procedures, methods, systems, processes, concepts, principles discoveries, or devices
- Information that is common property, with no original authorship, like calendars, tape measures, and rulers, as well as lists and tables taken from public domain sources

If you decide to register your work, you'll need to submit a registration form, a fee, and copies of your work. Visit the website of the copyrights office of the Library of Congress to make sure you have the most current registration form, and note that certain states have different registration form requirements. Mail the signed and completed order form, copies, and fee to:

Register of Copyrights
Copyright Office
Library of Congress
Washington D.C. 20559-6000

The response period is about sixteen weeks, upon which you'll receive a certificate of registration. As the author, you're able to copyright at any time, even after the work has been published. For books, the Copyright Office prefers hardcovers over paperbacks; however, electronic copies of books are preferred over printed books.

Acknowledgments

Many people helped develop and enhance the idea for this book, offering invaluable feedback and much-needed encouragement. In addition to the authors who inspired this book, the following people helped make it a reality.

I'd like to specifically thank the contributing authors Gordon Fredrickson, Patrick Mader, Robin Dedeker, DeAnne Sherman, Derek Wolden, Colleen Baldrica, Marilyn Jax, Tim Munkeby, Amy Recob, Deirdre Van Nest, Sara Jensen-Fritz, Paula Jones Johnson, Thea L. Zitzow, Susie Bazil, Gregg Proteaux, Ken Thurber, and Suzanne Ruff. Thank you for sharing your experiences as authors and especially for your honesty and candor. Your true accounts of the self-publishing experience are an invaluable addition to this book. It has been my ultimate pleasure knowing you and reading your books.

I'd also like to thank the following editors for their contributions: Amy Quale, Kellie Hultgren, Jennifer Manion, Molly Miller, April Michelle Davis, Joseph Moses, Matt Beier, Lily Coyle, and Hanna

Kjeldbjerg. Your critique, tireless editing, and insight helped beyond measure. Thank you for pushing me especially when I thought I was finished. Your push improved this manuscript beyond measure. I'm so grateful for your time and interest in helping me write this book. Your editorial eyes helped increase my confidence, and I could not have published this book without you.

The following designers gave more than I could have asked to help shape this book: Ryan Scheife of Mayfly Design and Jay Monroe of James Monroe Design. Thank you for answering my questions and for always being invaluable resources. You both are my anchors in the daily grind of book publishing, and I'm forever grateful for your patience, wonderful attitudes, and beautiful work.

Thank you to the Beaver's Pond Press staff (Tom Kerber, Heather Kerber, Matt Beier, Amy Quale, Lily Coyle, and Hanna Kjeldbjerg) for supporting this endeavor. You truly feel like my family, and this project was a special gift thanks to you.

Thanks to the following mentors, supporters, and dear friends: Milt "Beaver" Adams, Jordan Wiklund, Susan Adams Lloyd, Gary Mazzone, Rachel Anderson, Sara Lien, Bill and Gail Roddy, The Loft Literary Center, Teresa Thomas-Carroll, Women in Networking, Sam Ingram, Christy Eichers, Jasmine Stringer, Jenna Adams, Khaleelah Gilcreast, Erica McElroy, Janeen Carter, Carnell Cherry, Shayla Jackson, Andrea Cornett-Scott, Bob Grotjon, and Bob Hauserman.

Many thanks to my family for being the best base an author could have. To my husband Tomme Beevas, you inspire me every day, and I thank you from the bottom of my heart for your encouragement, delicious home-cooked meals, and limitless love. Thanks to my sisters and brothers (Matthew Brown, Justin Fennell, Markeda Brown, and

Kiara Hembry). You four are why I strive to do my best in all things. Thanks for being my motivators. Being your sister is one of the greatest blessings in my life. Mom, you taught me all I needed to know about survival—period. Thank you for being the kindest and most giving person in my world. Dad, the thought of you always makes me smile, and I needed that as I wrote this book. Thanks also to my stepfather Mark for all you've done for me.

Endnotes

1. NPR Books, "Barry Eisler's 'Detachment' From 'Legacy' Publishing," October 7, 2011, *NPR Books: Author Interviews*, http://www.npr.org/2011/10/07/141116856/barry-eislers-detachment-from-legacy-publishing.

2. Jeffrey Trachtenberg, "Authors Feel the Pinch as E-books Upend Book Publishing" *Wall Street Journal*, (2010).

3. Christina Katz, *Get Known Before the Book Deal: Use Your Personal Strengths to Grow an Author Platform*. (Cincinnati: Writer's Digest Books, 2008), 12.

4. Bruce Ross-Larson, *Edit Yourself: A Manual for Everyone Who Works With Words* (New York: W.W. Norton and Company, 1996), 41.

5. David Meerman Scott, *The New Rules of Marketing & PR: How to use News Releases, Blogs, Podcasting, Viral Marketing & Online Media to Reach Buyers Directly* (New Jersey: John Wiley & Sons, 2009), 145.

6. Thomas Woll, *Publishing for Profit: Successful Bottom-Line Management for Book Publishers* (Chicago: Chicago Review Press, 2002), 174-175.

7. Woll, *Publishing for Profit*, 279.

8. John Koetsier, "Electronic book sales doubled in 2011 (and the industry is just finding out now)", http://venturebeat.com/2012/07/18/electronic-book-sales-doubled-in-2011-and-the-industry-is-just-finding-out-now.

9. Gilles Biscos, "Digital Printing: Poised For Growth: A look at the trends behind the market's significant expansion," http://www.bookbusinessmag.com/article/digital-book-printing-poised-for-growth-a-look-industry-trends/.

10. Geoffrey A. Fowler and Marie C. Baca, "The ABCs of E-Reading." *The Wall Street Journal*, (2010): D1–D2.

11. Biscos.

12. Jackie Wong, "Genre-fiction fans quell hunger with e-books," http://www.straight. com/article-402353/vancouver/genrefiction-fans-quell-hunger-ebooks.

13. William E. Kassdorf, *The Columbia Guide to Digital Publishing*. (New York: Columbia University Press, 2003), 165.

14. Fowler and Baca, *Wall Street Journal*, D1–D2.

15. Albert N. Greco, *The Book Publishing Industry*. (Mahwah: Lawrence Erlbaum Associates, Inc., Publishers, 2005), 200.

16. Greco, *The Book Publishing Industry*, 141.

17. Greco, *The Book Publishing Industry*, 143.

18. Scott, *The New Rules of Marketing & PR*, 64.

19. Bryan Chick, "How a Self-Published Author Scored a Big New York Publisher," *ForeWord Magazine*, (2010): 64.

20. Mark Hachman, "Twitter Continues to Soar in Popularity, Site's Numbers Reveal," http://www.pcmag.com/article2/0,2817,2392658,00.asp.

Index

About the Author

Dara M. Beevas is a writer, editor, blogger, speaker, and indie author. As vice president of award-winning Beaver's Pond Press, she's mentored hundreds of authors through the publishing process.

Dara is a graduate of Mary Baldwin College and has a graduate degree in publishing from George Washington University. She's worked for the U.S. Chamber of Commerce and as an editor for the American Chemical Society. Her passion for the indie author revolution led her to launch Wise Ink, an online support community for authors. A native of the Washington, D.C. area, she currently lives in the Twin Cities with her husband Tomme.

Dara Beevas is available for keynote presentations and full-day seminars. She is a frequent speaker at trade shows and conferences, where she helps authors refine and polish content. Her presentations are a combination of humor, education, and inspiration. You can visit www.indieauthorbook.com for more information on her upcoming events. She's also reachable on LinkedIn, on the Indie Author Revolution Facebook fan page, and @darairene on Twitter.

About Beaver's Pond Press

Beaver's Pond Press is a strong supporter of Dara Beevas and of this book, which represents the democratization of the publishing process for authors everywhere. Since 1998, Beaver's Pond Press has guided nearly 1,000 authors in all genres through the publishing process. As a mentoring press, we work with and for our authors to achieve the greatness we know is within reach. Please visit our website to learn more about our company and services, and what we can do to help you achieve your dream of publication. For more information visit: www.beaverspondpress.com.